X

THE MIGHTY AFFAIR

Frontispiece

The presentation of the
Treaty of Union to Queen
Anne by the English and
Scottish Commissioners,
July 23, 1706. A drawing
by J. Gerhard Huck of
Dusseldorf engraved by
Valentine Green.

The Mighty Affair

HOW SCOTLAND LOST HER PARLIAMENT

Charles Hendry Dand

OLIVER & BOYD · EDINBURGH

First published 1972 by
Oliver and Boyd
Tweeddale Court
14 High Street
Edinburgh EH1 1YL
(A Division of Longman Group Ltd)

ISBN 0 05 002356 X

Printed in Great Britain by
Willmer Brothers Limited
Birkenhead

CONTENTS

ILLUSTRATIONS

Frontispiece—The presentation of the Treaty of Union to Queen Anne. (Reproduced by courtesy of the Trustees of the British Museum, London.)

Plate I—The Scottish Parliament in session. (Reproduced by courtesy of the National Museum of Antiquities of Scotland.)

Plate II—Parliament House, Edinburgh, as it was in 1707. (Reproduced by courtesy of the Rt. Hon. Lord Clyde, Lord President of the Court of Session.)

Plate III—JAMES DOUGLAS, 4th Duke of Hamilton. (Detail from portrait on loan to the Scottish National Portrait Gallery, reproduced by courtesy of His Grace the Duke of Hamilton and Brandon.) JAMES DOUGLAS, 2nd Duke of Queensberry. (Detail from a portrait by an unknown artist, reproduced by courtesy of the Scottish National Portrait Gallery.) JAMES OGILVY, 1st Earl of Seafield. (Detail of a portrait by Sir John B. de Medina, reproduced by courtesy of the Scottish National Portrait Gallery.) SIDNEY GODOLPHIN, 1st Earl of Godolphin. (From an engraving of a portrait by Sir Godfrey Kneller, reproduced by courtesy of the Mansell Collection.)

Plate IV—JOHN CAMPBELL, 2nd Duke of Argyll. (Detail of a portrait by William Aikman, reproduced by courtesy of the Scottish National Portrait Gallery.) JOHN MURRAY, 1st Duke of Atholl. (Detail of a portrait by Thomas Murray, reproduced by permission of His Grace The Duke of Atholl.) ANDREW FLETCHER OF SALTOUN. (Detail of a portrait by an unknown artist, reproduced by courtesy of the Scottish National Portrait Gallery.) JOHN HAMILTON, 2nd Lord Belhaven. (Detail from a portrait copied by John Medina, reproduced by courtesy of the Scottish National Portrait Gallery.)

Plate V—The last page of the Treaty of Union as signed by 26 Scottish and 27 English Commissioners on July 22, 1706.

Plate VI—Another page of signatures to the Treaty of Union. (Plates V and VI Crown Copyright, reproduced by courtesy of the Controller of Her Majesty's Stationery Office.)

PREFACE

The story of how the Scots lost the separate parliament many of them want to get back again has never been told for general readers. It is dismissed in a paragraph in the histories of Britain and only specialists in the period know the choleric and often ludicrous details of the drama that was enacted on both sides of the border.

In the opening decade of the eighteenth century, England was at war with Louis XIV. The government was terrified that the Scots would cast off rule from London, which they had resentfully accepted most of the time since the union of the crowns in 1603, and open England's back door to French invasion. The Scots were in a mood to make the break. The English were growing steadily richer and the Scots were desperately poor. They ascribed their poverty primarily to England's harsh refusal to allow them any share in her developing trade with the American colonies and the East. So enraged had they become that in 1703 they passed through their parliament an act to separate the Scottish crown again unless they were granted equal access to the sources of England's prosperity. The English parliament retaliated with an ultimatum that if the Scots had not committed themselves before Christmas 1705 to keep the same monarch as England, all trade between the countries would be stopped and Scotsmen venturing across the border would be treated as enemy aliens. Scots and English stood on the brink of war.

A few politicians on both sides set themselves to cool the tempers. The Scots persuaded their parliament to agree to negotiate and the English induced their parliament to withdraw the ultimatum. In 1706 thirty English and thirty-one Scots commissioners sat down in London to hammer out a treaty. The Englishmen viewed Scotland's separate parliament as a standing menace to their country's safety and were determined to destroy it. So they offered the Scots the trade equality they wanted plus £398 085 10s if they would give up their parliament. Twenty-six of the Scots thought the cash and an opportunity of riches a fair exchange and signed the treaty.

They had to get a majority for ratification in the Scottish parliament. More than a million Scots of all classes, practically the whole nation, hotly opposed the deal. They preached and prayed, petitioned and pamphleteered, raved and rioted. The twenty-six argued, intrigued, manoeuvred, bullied, and were believed to have bribed. After months of strenuous debate, during which they required the protection of troops against the fury of the Edinburgh mob, with reinforcements waiting across the border, they got their way by majorities of no more than thirty to forty of the three hundred lords and commoners who made up Scotland's single-chamber legislature.

Resistance to the treaty by English peers and M.P.s was less fierce. All they were being asked to do, apart from paying the cash, was to tolerate the presence among them of sixteen lords and forty-five commoners from Scotland. They despised and disliked Scots and abominated Presbyterians, but they need not be there to listen when the Scots spoke.

The mass of the English people took the new union with the Scots in their contemptuous stride and only remembered it when immigrant Scots obtruded on their attention. The Scots took half a century to begin to recover from the loss of their independence.

None of the men who brought about the union of the parliaments is venerated in England or Scotland. Although the treaty they engineered created the United Kingdom, no wreaths are placed on their graves on May 1, the day it came into being. School children are not taught their names. Neither country has ever celebrated a United Kingdom Day or a Union of the Parliaments Day. Yet the right to trade, fight and colonise alongside the English, for which the Scots commissioners swapped their country's parliament, freed the English from fear of being stabbed in the back and enabled Scots to play a part out of proportion to their numbers in the building of the British Empire. The empire has now all but vanished and the unity of the parliaments is threatened by the demands of Scots and Welsh for self-government. Before anything of the kind happens, the men who made the union – and the men who fought against it – deserve to have their memories taken out and the dust of more than two and a half centuries brushed away.

This book aims to do just that, to gather together in one fresh narrative events and incidents, exciting in their day and of great moment in their outcome, which have hitherto been available only in specialised accounts of the period and contemporary journals and memoirs. The greater part is concerned with the happenings of 1703–1707. To put these in perspective, however, the opening chapter tells briefly how James VI of Scotland made a personal conjunction with the English in 1603 and so laid a foundation for the later union of parliaments and peoples, and the second chapter glances at the tribulations which arose for both peoples, but especially for the Scots, from the attempt to balance two crowns – and two parliaments – on a single royal head.

It was Daniel Defoe who, in his *History of the Union of Great Britain,* called the successful negotiation of the treaty that extinguished Scotland's parliament 'this mighty affair'.

$$
\begin{array}{r}
16\overset{\text{\tiny 8}}{8}3 \\
6,9 \\
\hline
1114
\end{array}
$$

$$
160 \qquad
\begin{array}{r}
\overset{\text{\tiny 010}}{1603} \\
169 \\
\hline
1534
\end{array}
$$

1 The Uniting of the Crowns

For three centuries the English and the Scots fought and intrigued, wedded and bedded over the union of their countries. A Scots king died in battle, another of grief, and a Scots queen lost her head. For nearly half of the sixteenth century, to further their own ends, the French and Spanish courts and the Vatican strove to promote or prevent it. For the last decade of that century every Englishman with any kind of fortune to preserve or make racked his brains whether to hope for or fear it. In Edinburgh a king with eyes too big for his face, a tongue too large for his mouth, a beard too thin for his chin, clothes too full for his body, a body too heavy for his legs, a purse too small for his needs, a mind over-stuffed for the comfort of his wits, and a conceit of himself so gross even Scots laughed at it, agonised for thirty years over how God or he or anyone else could most speedily fulfil the undoubted divine intention that he should be the means of it. In the event it came quietly because a painstaking Englishman determined that it should and planned accordingly.

At a quarter to three in the morning of Thursday, March 24, 1603, after a reign of forty-five years in which England had become stable, powerful and prosperous and which had made her a marvel among the monarchs of her time, sixty-nine years old Queen Elizabeth died peacefully in Richmond Palace. For days London had silently waited the end. Church bells had stopped ringing. Trumpets had not been blown. Voices had been lowered. A great grief and a momentous question hung over all the England which the news had reached. The mother of a people was dying and with her a security to which they had become accustomed. A vast unknown lay before them but their faces, minds and nerves stayed frozen while she breathed.

An hour before noon a vital part of the question was answered. In London the heralds proclaimed Elizabeth's successor to be

1

James, King of Scotland. At long last there was to be a union between England and Scotland, a union in a person who had been invited by Elizabeth's Privy Council to put her crown on top of his own.

Whether it would stay there nobody could tell. Few in England knew what manner of man or king James was or would be, but somehow or other, in the way these things are done, a decision had been made. Nobody was surprised. It had been talked of for a long time as a likely possibility. The general reaction was relief that the matter appeared to have been settled and hope that a conflict might thereby be spared. No group of any size was disposed to make any murmur of opposition. That was that and they could return, most of them, to mourning their queen. The thoughts of the ambitious began to turn northwards. Thus it was throughout the country. As the news of the awesome death spread there followed quick upon it the reassuring news about James.

So, in his care for the peace of England and his own position, Robert Cecil, Elizabeth's astute Secretary of State, had planned it.

When the news reached Edinburgh it was digested with mixed feelings. The Scots were pleased and excited that their Jamie was to be king of England. It was a proper turning of the tables on the English for all the bloody efforts they had made to impose their kings on Scotland. They were relieved that the table-turning was apparently to be effected without more conflict and bloodshed. With difficulty they tried to comprehend that the threat of English invasion might be over. It was less agreeable that king and court at once engaged with indecent haste in packing up to quit the town. Little enough trade came to the Edinburgh merchants from Holyroodhouse, but it would be missed, and it was suddenly realised that there would be an eerie emptiness about life in a capital city that had no king to cheer or jeer at as the mood took it. The citizens of Edinburgh faced a rude demotion.

Queen Elizabeth died on Thursday. A letter from the English Privy Council arrived at Holyrood on Sunday. It assured James that in spite of their grief for their late queen the whole English people were overjoyed to have him as their king. The councillors were his to command and they implored him to let them see him with all possible speed.

James gave them their wish. He called together the leading

nobles living within a quick ride of Edinburgh, appointed a council to administer Scotland, made arrangements for the custody of his children, told his pregnant wife she could follow him at her leisure, and on Tuesday was off, the first Scot to justify Dr Johnson's remark that the noblest prospect which a Scotchman ever sees is the highroad that leads him to England.

If anyone had suggested to James that he should rule Scotland and England from Edinburgh and not from London he would have been given very short shrift. The possibility of remaining in Edinburgh never even crossed his mind. For him accession to the English crown was a glorious escape – escape from poverty, his own and Scotland's; escape from the humiliations he had endured since infancy at the hands of uncouth people, turbulent nobles, a rebellious and censorious Kirk, and the dead Elizabeth herself; escape from his horror of lethal steel and the threat of abduction or coercion; escape into a promised land of opulence, obedience, reverence for his exalted station, appreciation of his rare talents, and love of his most amiable person. No one in his suite, not even his wife, could know all that escape to England meant to James, but no one, not even the Presbyterian ministers who had never hesitated to tell him what they expected of him, thought of questioning or hindering his precipitate departure.

It was of no consequence what might happen to Scotland or its people through the move. Everyone knew, if they cared to think about it, that the English would not tolerate an absentee king. His presence among them was a *sine qua non* of any union and had been taken for granted. They had the larger country, a more numerous population, superior wealth, and a more important position in the world. No king with any pretensions to royal estate could dream of preferring little Edinburgh to swaggering London. The exercise of power and authority also demanded residence in London. It might be possible for James to keep from London as much control of Scotland as he had hitherto enjoyed; it would be quite impossible for him to rule England from Edinburgh as Elizabeth had ruled from London. The international situation was another factor. Whitehall and London were names to conjure with in the politics of Europe, which were extending to America, Africa and Asia. Holyrood and Edinburgh were no more than keys to the back-door of England, of some value when England's enemies were mounting a threat to her safety but otherwise small

beer in international diplomacy. James would not help his aspirations to cut a dash in the world by skulking in the back parts
of his domains and leaving its grander front uninhabited and
exposed to the machinations of his more established princely
rivals.

The Scots themselves took the change as much for granted as
the English. Common people were not given to challenging the
actions of kings unless prompted by their betters and to most of
the latter in Scotland the idea of exporting their king to England
was not wholly unattractive. If they were the kind to whom kings
and courts mattered and thought they had the means and
manners to consort with the English, Whitehall and Richmond
offered more promise than Holyrood and Falkland. If, for one
reason or another, they had failed to make good at Holyrood or
were indifferent to royal favour, the farther away the king was the
louder they could crow on their own dung-hills without possible
interference from him. Nor would any of the clergy or members
of the powerful Presbyterian Kirk weep because James was leaving
them. In their view the government of the Kirk and the interpretation and application of its doctrine were matters to be
decided by debate and vote among themselves, with God sitting
neutral in the chair and the Bible as the rule-book. James had no
quarrel with their basic dogma but he regarded it as his prerogative by divine appointment to hand down the interpretations and
the government, assisted by the episcopacy of his own choosing.
So far the struggle had been inconclusive. No doubt it irked the
more rabid among the clergy that he was escaping from them to
a country where he could walk straight to the seat he had been
demanding, and they viewed it as another of Satan's favours to
his own. On the other hand, it could be God's curious way of
ridding them of such interference. It might be an instance where
God and the devil were not exactly crossing each other's
purposes. At least, it would give them a breathing-space of which
they could make vociferous use. The smaller number of Scots
Episcopalians were cheered by the thought of a link with their
English co-religionists and even the Catholics entertained hopes
that God might have some surprise for them.

So James left Edinburgh without any more incommoding
thought on his mind than that the money in his pocket was not
calculated to take him any farther than Berwick. It had been

hard to raise even that. Happily there was gold across the border. God grant he encounter it soon!

The validity of his claim by right of blood to the English crown was substantial. Both his mother and his father were grandchildren of Henry VII's elder daughter, Margaret, and his double descent from the first Tudor gave him precedence over others of that seed. There had been four threats to it, however. One, Henry VIII had left a will disinheriting his sister Margaret's children and vesting the succession, if his own children died childless, in the issue of his younger sister Mary, who had a great-grandson, Lord Beauchamp. Fortunately for James, Beauchamp was not thought likely by anybody to be much of a king, and as there was some doubt whether his parents' marriage had been legal there had been no great desire to give him the benefit of the will unless Elizabeth wished it. Two, there were tales about James's mother, Mary, Queen of Scots, and the Italian Rizzio. Nobody would want James if he were a bastard. Three, in English eyes James was as much a foreigner as if he had been born in France or Norway and since under common law no alien could inherit land in England it might be argued that no alien could inherit England itself. It was to overcome this obstacle that James repeatedly pleaded with Elizabeth to disregard his Scottish birth and make an Englishman of him, by treating him as the heir of his English father's English father and giving him the family estates which she had taken to herself. When she refused he argued that she had anglified him by giving him an annual pension in lieu of the estates. The point was of more importance because there was an English-born claimant of the same line of descent from Henry VII as himself, young Arabella Stuart, his cousin, daughter of his father's brother Charles. If being an alien or a reputed bastard made him unacceptable, and Henry's will were ignored, the crown would be Arabella's.

The fourth and perhaps biggest threat was an act of the English parliament passed in 1584 declaring forfeit all claims to the crown of persons who plotted against the life of Elizabeth. It had been aimed primarily at James's mother, who was executed three years later for that very crime. James had tried hard to keep out of involvement in any conspiracy that went as far as assassination, but he could never be sure that some of the conspirators with whom he flirted would not cross the banned line, or that someone would not make false charges against him to spoil his chances. It had also been open to anyone to maintain that his claim had been forfeited through his mother's offence.

The only person who could have resolved the difficulties and put an end to his years of suspense was Elizabeth and he had never ceased to urge her to announce him as her accepted successor. The farthest she had ever gone had been to undertake to do nothing to injure his prospects provided he did nothing to provoke her. It had been impossible for the impatient James to be content with this dubious assurance. He knew there was enough on the record to allow her to bilk him if she felt inclined, and it was clear she had no love for him from the way she never lost an opportunity of hectoring him and lecturing him about his inadequacies. If neither she nor God would help him, he had to help himself and risk the provocations.

He had sunk pretty low in his desperation to quit Scotland for England. He had manoeuvred and intrigued, cringed and wheedled, argued and expostulated, shifted and shuffled, equivocated and prevaricated, double-dealt and double-crossed everybody, including his own mother, to enlist support for his claim to the crown and aid to take it by force should anyone try to cheat him of it. He had earned the reputation of a fool and a bounder in every court in Europe, but twenty years of panting after the English crown did him no good. Suddenly in 1601 his luck turned. Robert Cecil, Elizabeth's Secretary of State, decided that the time had come to control his reckless plungings, calm the distracted creature down, and prepare the way for him to fulfil his destiny in an orderly fashion.

Cecil was moved by a number of considerations. He held the power in England under Elizabeth. She was no longer the woman she had been. She was nearing seventy, her health was unpredictable, and she had had no heart for living since sending to the scaffold the Earl of Essex, the last of her loves. It had become imperative that England – Cecil at least – should prepare for her death and this meant settling the question of the succession. Cecil's thought in turning to James was to do the right thing for the future of England and the monarchy. If England's security and prosperity were to be maintained, there must be no hiatus in the grip of the crown on all English affairs. The wearer must be strong and sensible and have an unquestionable right to it. James was neither strong nor sensible but it was undeniable that Henry VII's blood flowed in his veins. At the same time, he was not a weakling and stronger than Arabella Stuart was likely to be. He was not English, but a Scot was nearer to being English than a Spaniard. He was a Protestant by conviction and Cecil was convinced that a secure England must be a Protestant England. His assumption of the English as well as the Scottish crown would close the vulnerable back door to England which might be thrown wide open if he were robbed of his expectations. The personality of the man apart, the arguments were all in favour of James.

Only one thing was needed to give James strength and sense – the strength and sense of Cecil himself. They were nearly of an age – James thirty-seven, he forty. Under his guiding hand James might make a good enough king of England. In any case, there was no better available. It would take all his time and energy for the rest of his life but he was used to long hours of unsparing toil and what else should he live for, a friendless widower with a curved spine, accustomed to the exercise of power and having the will to use it for the good of his country? He moved to bring James under his control.

The move was made to a diplomatic mission James had sent to London to get him out of certain embarrassments that had arisen in the course of the Essex treason trials. Cecil invited the ambassadors to a secret meeting and announced that if James would undertake to allow Elizabeth to complete her reign undisturbed and unthreatened in any way, and also to keep absolutely secret any communications that might pass between them, he would undertake to secure James's peaceful accession to the throne when Elizabeth died. Elizabeth must not be bullied or irritated. She must be wooed and he would show James how. If a whisper got out that James and he were in correspondence, he had ten thousand enemies who would shout it to Elizabeth. Let James be known as Cecil's king and half England would start working to thwart them. But without him no one in England or out of it could guarantee James anything. When the time came James could rely on him to have pulled all the strings.

The ambassadors were properly impressed. They swore themselves to secrecy and undertook to use all their influence on James.

Cecil gave them a letter to take back to James and a cipher to be used in correspondence. No names were to be mentioned, only numbers. Cecil himself would be 10, the Earl of Mar (leader of the Scottish ambassadors) 20, Elizabeth 24, and James would be designated 30.

It worked out as Cecil had planned. James was remarkably well-behaved. Under Cecil's tuition he began to make advances to Elizabeth, assuring her of his admiration and affection, stressing the sincerity of his wishes for her continued health and happiness of mind, swearing his innocence of any desire to encroach upon her preserves. Elizabeth may have wondered at the change in his attitude but probably put it down to Anno Domini – the Scottish urchin, as she had called him, was at last growing up and she was conscious of her own age. Anyhow, she professed her pleasure at finding him so amenable. She called him her 'dear brother'. James vowed ecstatically that her letters made him happier than if he had won the Golden Fleece. The two hypocrites tossed endearments across the border to one another but there may have been some genuine warmth on both sides. Elizabeth may have turned in a last extremity to showing a little affection towards her least risky successor, while James may have been able to transfer some of his passion for the crown into a sympathy with its declining wearer – in his moments of literary composition, at least. When the loving letter had been signed and sealed he could return, without consciousness of inconsistency, to his prayers for her speedy decease.

Once he felt confident he had James under control Cecil went to work on other members of Elizabeth's Privy Council. His case was that there was less risk of the golden today becoming an uncertain and cloudy tomorrow under James than under anyone else. If they all stuck together, James could mount the throne in peace as no other claimant could, and from peace within the realm they all had least to fear. If they stuck together for James, they might earn a joint reward from him, keep out aspiring outsiders, defend the club which had been congenial to them all. The arguments seemed to be in favour and in Cecil's persuasive tones they prevailed.

All that remained to be done was to make sure that when the crucial moment came nothing should happen to sound a rallying call for the disaffected in the population. The steps were taken as soon as it appeared that Elizabeth would not recover from her illness. London was placed under guard and throughout the country the Justices of the Peace were warned to be on the alert to suppress any threat of a disturbance, while the captains of garrisons were ordered to have forces ready to proceed immediately to the aid of any magistrates who might require it. A watch was kept at sea along the south-east coast in case any desperadoes from the Spanish Netherlands might be tempted to try a landing, and all traffic with the continent was carefully screened against subversive incomers. Known malcontents were rounded up and Cecil's political spies circulated actively in search of possible trouble-makers.

The truth was that the mass of the English were indifferent to James, as a person or as a monarch. Few knew anything about him, except that he lived remotely to the north of them among a wilder people called Scots whom they feared, disliked, despised or were quite unacquainted with, according to their distance from them, and that he had a claim by right of descent to rule over them which nobody seemed very much disposed to dispute. If it were God's will to impose a Scot on them, and their betters were not objecting, they need not withhold their mute amens. In any case, nobody was asking them and they were hoping not to be asked, for if they were, if there were a choice, all their history told them that trouble would ensue and most of them were anxious to avoid that.

The mood was much the same up and down the social scale, varying only with the degree of satisfaction with things as they were. Cecil's arguments to his fellow-councillors had percolated down through all the lesser powers in town and country: those who were prospering and were averse to hazardous change should opt for James.

The security grip imposed, a form of proclamation of James's impending accession was drawn up and sent off for his approval. All hope of the Queen's recovery had been abandoned. It was still desirable however, to obtain from her, if at all possible, her acquiescence in their choice. If she could signify that she knew and had no objection, it would put a constitutional seal on their selection and remove the possibility of any charge that they had usurped the royal prerogative. They assembled at her bedside and spoke gently to her of their need to know her mind. As from a long

way off she appeared to understand and struggled to speak. Cecil
bowed low over her, straining to hear. The words came cryptically,
oracularly, barely audibly through her twisting lips. 'Who should
succeed me but a king?' she whispered. The members of the
council were puzzled. Was it an answer or another evasion? Cecil
pressed for a clarification. 'Who but our cousin of Scotland?' she
moaned impatiently as if the issue had never been in doubt. 'I pray
you trouble me no more.'

Cecil had fulfilled his promise.

Any anxieties James may have had about his reception by the
English were relieved from the moment he arrived at the gates of
Berwick. His departure from Edinburgh had been so sudden and
swift that the citizens of the border fortress town were given no
time to mount any pageantry appropriate to so momentous an
occasion as the appearance in their midst of a brand new
sovereign, an angel of peace miraculously descending from the
hills of their ancient enemies to end the pillage, arson and bloodshed which they had endured and inflicted for so many centuries.
They offered instead a welcome calculated to appeal to any Scot
and meeting bankrupt James's most desperate need – a purse of
gold. He glowed with joy. This was England as he had expected it
to be and his first loyal subjects could not have found a quicker
way to his heart.

His satisfaction grew with every mile. Every village church
rang its bell and parson and people came out to cheer. Country
roads were lined with gawking peasants from all the parishes
within a day's walking distance. The mayor and corporation of
every town presented an address of welcome and some of them
a masque. But the highlights of the progress were the stops in the
houses of the nobles and richer gentry who vied with one another
in banquets, comforts and entertainments for their king. The
number of attendant nobles and gentlemen had been modest when
he left Edinburgh but was swelled every day by Scots hurrying
south after him and English hastening northwards to meet him,
all bent on getting close while he might still be hot with the
pleasure of his new-found power and ready to show it in a generous
bestowal of titles, offices and more tangible marks of favour. Soon
there were over a thousand clamorous place-seekers in the train
that wound through England after him, competing at every turn

for his attention and falling like locusts on the food and lodging which his hosts felt compelled to provide for them, not knowing whom it was safe to refuse among the rabble.

In vain James ordered the Scots among them who were not his official attendants to go back home again. They knew their only hope of preferment or profit lay where the king was and they were sure that would not be in Scotland if he could help it. All they were seeing of England convinced them that James and his successors would never return to Edinburgh except for the briefest possible visits. They were determined to hang on to him like leeches, so long at least as the food was free in England. And Englishmen who had felt themselves starved of their deserts under Elizabeth's tight control of patronage could not wait passively at home while their brasher fellows were thrusting for the pickings.

The nearer James approached London, the larger became the welcoming crowds and the more magnificent the hospitality his hosts showered on him. Lord Burghley, Cecil's elder brother, staged a show at Burghley House which was as 'rich as if it had been furnished at the charges of an emperor'. Twelve miles out of London the host was Cecil himself, at Theobalds, the house to which he had devoted any time and energy he could spare from running England, and all the money that came his way. Here James met for the first time the members of his English Privy Council and made light of their difficulties in understanding his Scots tongue, reminding them that it was a language with as good a pedigree as their own, and cracked a few jokes in Latin and French to demonstrate his fitness to shine in any company of scholars and gentlemen. The Lord Mayor of London, accompanied by five hundred splendidly attired citizens on horseback, met him at Stamford Hill. The programme should have continued with a state entry into the City of London, the arrival of Queen Anne and the children who had followed him down through England in a second round of hospitality, ceremonial greetings and favour-hunting, and the most magnificent coronation England had known.

But James's luck was turning sour. Providence upset the arrangements by afflicting London with an outbreak of plague. For a couple of months he had to kill time by visiting his new palaces at Greenwich, Windsor and Whitehall, and touring in the home counties, while the plague death rate climbed to seven hundred persons a week. When the coronation was solemnised on July 25, Westminster Abbey was nearly empty, and the crown he had so long coveted was placed on his head with no more pomp and pageantry than if the ceremony had taken place in the shabby Scotland he had so joyfully abandoned. It was a sad anti-climax to the honeymoon which had begun so auspiciously with the purse of gold at Berwick.

So transpired the first union of England and Scotland. It had taken place, not because the English wanted to join up with the Scots or the Scots with the English, but because England had a void to fill and the man who wore the crown of Scotland was the most generally acceptable candidate to fill it. It was a union of crowns and no more. Nothing was changed in the formal relationships of the two countries except that for the time being they were both to have the same king.

Of course, both the English and the Scots expected that under the same king the two nations would henceforth be at peace with one another. There would, at least, be no armed invasions or raids, and since the enemies of the king of England would be enemies of the king of Scotland too, the latter would no longer blackmail the former by threatening to allow his country to be used as a base for war on England or subversive activities. The border areas were almost immediately affected by the anticipation of a new law and order which the king with two crowns would wish to enforce. The border would remain and the extent to which it might be freely crossed had not been determined, but neither the king of Scotland nor the king of England would any longer have blind eyes or deaf ears to turn when it was crossed by bands of armed men who robbed, murdered and burned as a way of life. The Scots traders were entertaining hopes that the frontier would go down and that they would enjoy free access to English goods and markets and the rich trade which the English were beginning to develop with India and America. Surely, they were starting to tell themselves, they would be entitled to something from the English in exchange for their king. But this was not how the English were seeing the union. They were willing in their own interests to take a Scotsman for their king with any ancillary benefits the adoption might bring them but they were certainly not contemplating admitting Scots to their bosoms or their counting-houses.

Disappointing though his coronation ceremony had been, James had ample reason to congratulate himself on the success of his take-over of England. Everywhere he had been hailed and treated as a great king should be. For the first time in his life he had been able to behave in a truly kingly way. He had spent over £10 000 of English money on the way south and had lavishly distributed another £14 000 in gifts to those who pleased him. He had made knights, barons and councillors. He had experienced as never before the joys of wealth and power. He believed the English were as pleased with him as he with them. On the whole the English were genuinely satisfied with what they had seen of the prize they had drawn out of heredity's lucky-bag. The more sophisticated found his manners crude and his approach altogether of a homelier kind than seemed proper in royalty, but they had to agree that he could behave with dignity when occasion demanded and had intelligence above their own average. Even his appearance, 'neither fat nor thin, of full vitality, neither too large nor too small', met with approbation. 'In the whole man he was not uncomely', wrote a scrupulous commentator, advancing a cautious hand towards the bandwagon of flattery on which statesmen, diplomats, clergy and poets were all vociferously clambering. The whole nation donned rose-coloured spectacles through which to view their king, grateful because the competition appeared to have ceded him victory without even a spark of a struggle, grateful that no carpers seemed to want to cloud the outlook with sinister hints and prophecies, grateful above all that he was a king, a man, a male with heirs of his body already in evidence, and for the assurances that fact promised for the future. No king had ever before mounted the throne of England with so much expression of unreserved goodwill.

In one thing James fell short of what was being expected of him. From his childhood he had hated crowds. In Scotland they had always meant danger. He could not wholly overcome this aversion even when the populations of whole English towns were tumbling over one another to call down blessings on him. He was easily bored with repetitious ceremonial and when the novelty of worshipping mobs had worn off he became impatient and tried to cut short the ordeals. When criticisms of his frowns were reported to him he asked angrily what the populace demanded of him. It was explained that all they wanted was to see as much of him as possible. 'God's wounds!' he is said to have shouted, 'then I will pull down my breeches and they shall also see my arse!'

The English were to see rather a lot of that aspect of him in the years to come.

2 The Disunited Kingdoms

Nothing in England or Scotland was constitutionally changed by the event of 1603. Both countries retained their separate Privy Councils, parliaments, law courts, churches, legislation and taxation. Neither Scots nor English obtained any rights or privileges in each other's countries other than posts and honours that might be conferred on them by the personal gift of the king. Trade in each country continued to be protected against the other and it was a punishable offence for a Scot to try to trade with an English colony. He could, however, trade with France or any other country with which England might go to war. The acts of the king and his parliament in one country did not commit him and his parliament in the other. In theory the Scots lost nothing of their independence by the union of the crowns and the English never gave a thought to the possibility of losing anything of theirs. James had come to them.

To give James his due he tried to effect a closer union between his two peoples. 'What God hath conjoined,' he told the English in his first address to their parliament, 'let no man separate. I am the Husband and all the whole Isle is my lawful wife. I am the Head and it is my Body. I am the Shepherd and it is my Flock. I hope, therefore, no man will be so unreasonable as to think that I, that am a Christian King under the Gospel, should be a Polygamist and Husband to two Wives; that I, being the Head, should have a divided and monstrous Body; or that, being the Shepherd to so fair a flock (whose fold hath no wall to hedge it but the four seas) should have my Flock parted in two. And as God hath made Scotland the one half of this Isle to enjoy my birth and the first and most imperfect half of my life, and you here to enjoy the perfect and the last half thereof, so can I not think that any would be so injurious to me as to cut asunder the one half of me from the other.'

He proposed that he should be styled King of Great Britain and Ireland, that there should be one flag combining the crosses of St George and St Andrew, that trade should be free between the two countries, and that all his subjects should enjoy equal citizenship rights on both sides of the border. The title and the Union Jack he obtained by exercising the royal prerogative and joint citizenship by a decision of the courts in England and a statute in Scotland. But he failed completely to persuade the English to agree to any Scottish share in their much more profitable trade. The Scots could come into England if the judges said they could not be kept out – no sane Englishman had any desire to enter Scotland – but they would not be encouraged; they were definitely not to be allowed to poach on English preserves. James did not feel the pain in the Scots half of his monstrous and divided Body for long; it contained neither his heart nor his belly.

Unhappily his efforts for Scotland proved disastrous. Freedom of entry into England for the Scots without freedom of trade between the countries gave Scotland nothing but a licence to bleed herself into a pernicious economic and political anaemia through the export of her most ambitious and enterprising citizens. The removal of king and court to London reduced Scotland to the level of an international nonentity. Nobody came any longer from abroad as there was no worthwhile business of any kind to attract visitors. All the nobility and gentry who felt the need to be in the swim of national, international or society affairs went off to London either permanently or for as long a time each year as they could afford. All the money they could squeeze out of their estates was spent there on efforts to live up to the English levels of luxury and magnificence, beggaring the Scots traders and craftsmen who had depended on them for a living and enhancing the profits of their English counterparts. This in turn either drew south the younger and more adventurous Scots, who began to find themselves without employment or prospects, or sent them off to Europe in search of a livelihood, since the growing English overseas trading and colonial enterprises were barred to them apart from James's pet scheme for the Protestant development of Ulster. The first result of union was to encourage the Scots to bankrupt altogether their already impoverished country.

Scotland still had her own parliament. But the Scottish parliament was far from being the influential voice of the landlords and the merchants into which the English parliament had developed under Elizabeth. It had never been much more than a rubber-stamp for any ukases which the monarch found himself strong enough to put before it and which were submitted through the Committee of the Articles. Bills prepared by the Committee were not debated by parliament, merely accepted or rejected.

Union helped the king with the two crowns to secure approving majorities in the Scottish parliament when it did meet. Aspiring Scottish nobles and gentlemen could get nowhere without his favour since he was no longer close enough to be bullied. A prerequisite of any preferment was to cast an affirmative vote for everything that came up from the Committee of the Articles. Those who wanted preferment could also render themselves more acceptable by switching from Presbyterianism to support of the episcopal church government which James was determined to thrust on Scotland or, at least, by taking no part in opposition to it. An effect of the union, therefore, was to keep Scotland well behind England in the growth of parliament as an instrument for the effective participation of any section of the people in the business of government. The fault, of course, lay as much with the Scots themselves as with dictator James. Too many of them were only too willing to sell their birthright of Scottish freedom for a mess of English pottage. It should be remembered, however, that while freedom and parliament had developed some synonymity in England, the Scots in James's time had not yet begun to see in the idea of a constitutional parliament a means of satisfying an urge towards democracy which was much stronger than that of the English. The democratic freedom early seventeenth-century Scots had set their hearts on reposed in the machinery governing their Kirk with its presbyteries, synods and General Assembly, and not at all in their parliament.

The only resistance James met with in running Scotland by remote control was in his efforts to make the stiff-legged Scots kneel in church to receive communion, to observe Christmas and Easter, and to be confirmed by bishops, all as the English were wont to do in the church of which he was now the acknowledged and enraptured head. The reaction was so violent that the effort had to be abandoned. The Scots preserved a measure of independence at the grassroots of their kirkyards which they lost to London higher up.

The chief consequences to England of the union with James were an abrupt termination of the reverence for the monarchy which had begun with the seventh and eighth Henrys and culminated in the popular worship of Elizabeth, an acceleration of the national consciousness of the possibilities of parliament as an instrument of government by debate and consent, and a sudden decline in the country's influence in international affairs. All of these were the opposite of James's desires and were the result of his utter inability to understand what he had taken on with the crown of England.

He upset his middle-class English subjects because he knew nothing of the political and legal history of England and tossed aside as useless lumber the fundamental laws of the realm and the privileges and precedents for which their fathers had struggled and to which they attached so much importance. He upset Anglicans and Puritans by his vacillations over the Catholics. He upset the merchants and seafarers because he had no interest in the sea and neglected to maintain the fleet that gave England control of the Channel and its approaches. He upset the influential political families by his attachment to upstart favourites whom he allowed to run the country for him. He upset nearly everybody by crawling to the Spaniards and trying to marry his son and heir to the Infanta. In short, by the time James died he had done just about everything he could to make the English wonder what sins they had committed for God and Cecil to have inflicted him upon them.

Nevertheless, the union was less damaging to the English than to the Scots. While the Scots were growing poorer, thanks to the union, the English were steadily growing richer in spite of it. The prosperous courses in agriculture, industry and trade on which they had set themselves in the previous reign continued, since James did not interfere with them. Trade with Spanish America was still reserved officially for Spaniards and the Portuguese did their best to prevent Englishmen from trading on the coasts of Africa and in the East Indies; but English sailors braved James's displeasure to find their own ways of enrichment at the expense of the Spaniards, and the English East India Company armed its ships and forced its way into the Asian markets. Englishmen were starting to colonise North America. The trade with Russia which Elizabethans had opened up was lost to the Dutch but, for what it was worth, there was the money citizens of the new Great Britain were bringing in from Scotland. All in all, the English were doing better than ever before and from most of their money-making Scots were excluded.

Conflict between crown and parliament might well have arisen in England during the sixteen hundreds if there had been no union and no James. The growth of parliamentary government was a road on which English feet were set. But the steps might have been slower, more tentative and less thundering without James to hurry them on by his vanities and stupidities. The Elizabethans had been only half-consciously feeling their way to-wards a method of government so far unknown and untried in the world. James forced them to think furiously about it, with disastrous consequences to his son and successor.

The first union of the crowns of England and Scotland was rudely severed in 1649 by the stroke of a masked headsman.

Both countries waged civil war against autocrat Charles I but each in its separate way. England's war was for parliament against king, Scotland's for Kirk against king. In 1641 the Presbyterian Covenanters forced Charles to agree that future appointments as Privy Councillors, officers of state, and judges would be made on the advice and with the approval of parliament, in which they had, for the time being, a majority. They were less concerned, how-ever, with establishing the authority of parliament than they were with protecting the Kirk, and twenty years later, when there were fewer Presbyterian zealots in the House, the members supinely re-stored to Charles II the powers wrested from his father, and the Scottish parliament returned to its traditional role of approving legislation put before it by the Committee of the Articles and the Privy Council.

When Charles was beheaded the two countries were as far apart as ever they had been before the union. England terminated its war against Charles by becoming a republic, Scotland by clinging to monarchy in the person of another Charles. The split was inevitable because the two countries had had nothing in common in the forty-six years but the head on which the two crowns sat.

The Scots Kirk men fought Charles as king of Scotland at their own expense but before they would fight him as king of

England they demanded that their expenses should be paid. The English accepted their aid but did not pay for it, so when the Scots took the luckless Charles prisoner they conveniently forgot he was king of Scotland and sold him to the English for four-fifths of the half-million they reckoned they had spent in helping the Parliamentarians to win battles on English soil. However, when the English executed Charles, the Scots were furious that the head that wore their crown had been axed without their permission, and they immediately crowned his son Charles to assert their complete dissociation from England.

In their civil war contacts Scots Presbyterians and English Puritans became as much objects of hatred to each other as they both were to Episcopalians. Stiff-minded themselves, the English Puritans found the Scots Presbyterians to be granitic in their intolerances. When the Puritan extremists executed Charles, outraged nationalist pride and sentimentality inflamed the resentments of the Scots. They had had no love themselves for the last three representatives of their Stuart royal house but even the most fervent Presbyterians had no objections to monarchy as such. They had always been prepared to tolerate kings and queens so long as they did not interfere with the Kirk. Charles had interfered, hence their rebellion against him. But regicide was going too far and the victim of the crime was not only a Scot by birth and descent but a Stuart and their king. So, having first protected the Kirk by asking the new Charles to sign a covenant to defend it, they crowned him at Scone and made ready to do losing battle with the great Cromwell and his Ironsides.

Cromwell gave England and Scotland the completer unity James had desired, and been denied, for the two halves of his Body. It took him not much more than a year to overcome the Scottish resistance. In place of the broken union of the crowns he substituted by force a union of the countries. It was a union of conquest and military occupation. He effected also a union of the parliaments, half a century before the date in the history books. What he did not achieve was any closer union of the peoples.

The Scottish crown was formally abolished and delegates were formally summoned to accept a tender of union with England. In 1654 thirty Scotsmen were selected to represent the country in a parliament of four hundred and sixty members at Westminster. All trade barriers between the countries were torn

PLATE I

The upper part of this plate from Nicolas de Gueudeville's *Atlas Historique*, published in 1721, is the only known illustration of the Scottish Parliament in session. It shows the 1660–1690 seating of the officers of state, bishops, nobility, and commoners without pretending to exactness of numbers. (No bishops sat in the Scottish Parliament after 1690.) The lower half depicts "The Riding" from Holyroodhouse to Parliament House.

PLATE II

Parliament House, Edinburgh, as it was in 1707. Built in 1639, its facade was altered to its present appearance in the early nineteenth century. The equestrian statue of Charles II was erected in 1685.

down. This was the only thing the Scots had ever wanted of union, but it did them no good. The time it lasted was too short and there was no capital for investment in trade. The burden of the taxation Cromwell imposed to pay for his garrisons was so heavy for a poor country that it was almost reduced to bankruptcy. Even the officers of the occupation army commiserated with the wretched Scots. The hatred of the occupied Scots for the occupying English was intensified by the apparent impossibility of throwing off a yoke clamped on their necks with devastating military skill. It meant nothing to them, of course, that England was also enduring military occupation under soldiers and generals of the same army. The English were being brow-beaten by other Englishmen, they by foreigners. The thirty Scottish members of the parliament at Westminster added insult to the injuries; they were quislings. In one respect only was Cromwell ready to relax the grip. He offered freedom of worship to all except Roman Catholics and Episcopalians. It was the one question on which the cowed Scots Kirk stood up to him. They would have freedom of worship only for Presbyterians. 'In the bowels of Christ', roared the exasperated Cromwell, 'think it possible you may be mistaken!' Even the famous plea to the innards of divinity could not move them. He did as James and Charles had done before him, dismissing the General Assembly and forbidding it to meet again. The Kirk enjoyed, however, the freedom of worship it denied to others, so the Scots were left content in the one thing that would have roused them to more rebellion, however suicidal.

All that Cromwell's total union of England and Scotland meant to the English was that the key of their back-door dangled safely from the Protector's belt.

The Scots rejoiced even more than the English over the second Charles's return from exile, but their joy was short-lived. There had been little of the Scot in the first Charles and there was none in his successor. Nor were there any Scotswomen among his many mistresses. Nobody wanted Cromwell's one country and one parliament so his unity was dissolved, and with it went his free trade. Scotsmen were again barred from any share in the profitable commerce of the Indies and the Americas. The whole machinery of separate Scottish government was restored, including the packed Committee of the Articles. The first Scottish acts of the new reign brought back bishops and took from congregations their democratic right to elect their ministers. These were to be selected by landowners and approved by the bishops.

The answer of the Scots was to go on a religious strike. Some three hundred ministers refused to seek the patronage of the landlords and abandoned their churches and manses. Loyal members of their congregations declined to enter the places of worship and services were held in barns and kitchens, in the fields and on the hillsides. Troops ranged the countryside in search of secret meeting-places and hunted down the recusant ministers. Imprisonment, torture and death were imposed. In 1666 the persecuted Covenanters were driven to retaliate with an armed march on Edinburgh but were routed. Their leaders were hanged. Concentration camps were established in places like the Bass Rock in the Firth of Forth, where hundreds died of harsh treatment and disease. Many were executed or died under torture. The brutal repression, which lasted for more than twenty years, bit deep into the national memory of Scotland and gave Presbyterianism a roll of heroes and martyrs. It started Scottish emigration to the West Indies and America. Ship captains engaged in illegal trade from Scottish ports with the English colonists gave passages to able-bodied refugee Covenanters, who sold themselves to the colonists for periods of slavery to raise the money for their fares.

It also split the Kirk into a minority, whose stern consciences permitted no compromise with an alien and idolatrous authority, and a larger number of weaker brethren who, to save their skins or lands, or because the extremists of their faith frightened them as much as the royal dragoons, sought a means of reconciling the torments of the next world with the pains of this one. The split had an important consequence. It reduced the domination of the bigots over the attitudes of Kirk and country and the voice of the Hebrew prophets was no longer the only one heard in the land.

Charles was content with a last-minute avowel of Roman Catholicism on his death-bed. His brother James's open determination to lead both his kingdoms willy-nilly back to Rome lost him both his crowns. Oddly enough, the Scots, whose hatred of everything Popish much exceeded the antipathies of the English, took James's first pro-Catholic moves very quietly. They were saved the need of any action on their own by the English. Stung by James's deafness to the protestations of church and parliament, and menaced by infiltration of Catholic troops from Ireland and possible invasion from France, the English struck out for Protest-antism by ousting James in favour of his daughter Mary and her stoutly Protestant husband, William of Orange.

In both his countries James lost his crown more quickly than he need have by his precipitate flight to France. Many English-men who were uneasy about him, or opposing him, would not so speedily have consented to the deposition and replacement of one whom they viewed as occupying the throne by divine right, had James not deserted them as soon as he learned the strength of William's forces and sought refuge with Louis XIV of France. Memories of the Civil War were still very much alive and the Restoration had not healed all the psychological and material wounds. There was a general reluctance to take up the sword again and James's indecent departure, Mary's participation in the divine right as his daughter, and William's willingness to treat all who came over to him as English gentlemen, combined to make acceptance of the new rule, whether qualified or unqualified, genuine or feigned, easy for everybody. Louis set up James, his second wife, and their infant son in a court of their own at St Germains, in a palace he had used before he built Versailles, and for the next two decades those who had given qualified or feigned allegiance to William and Mary led double lives by cor-responding, more or less secretly, with members of the St Germains court and drinking private toasts to the king across the water. In the first of these practices they were joined by not a few of those who professed to give William unqualified support, even some of the king's ministers and generals. Louis treated James most generously, giving him precedence over every Frenchman but him-self when he visited Versailles. At James's deathbed in 1701 he announced his acknowledgment of the son, now thirteen years old, as King of England, Scotland and Ireland and forced Queen Anne to end the peace France had patched up four years earlier with King William.

William's arrival and James's flight left the Scots with little option but to follow the English lead. Presbyterian Scotland could not be less anti-Catholic than Episcopalian England. Mary was a Stuart, so the national pride need not be hurt, and the Dutchman was the acknowledged Protestant champion of Europe. In choosing William the English Whig party were asserting human right against divine right in the disposal of crowns, the authority

B

of parliament alongside that of the king, and, for the reasons just stated, most of the English Tories had acquiesced. Some Scots nobles were quick, because of their principles, to pledge allegiance to William, others vied with them for reasons of political shrewdness and ambition. On the whole, however, Scots were slower than the English to prefer the foreigner with a Stuart wife to a king with the full Stuart blood royal. Highland chiefs and their clansmen were for James, either because they were Catholics or Episcopalians or unswayed by religion, or simply because they were hereditary enemies of the Campbells who acknowledged the Presbyterian Earl of Argyll as their paramount chief, and Argyll was backing William. Covenanters, Cameronians, and other extreme Presbyterians were for William because of the oppression they had endured under James. Most others were uncertain how they ought to go.

Under Charles II and James II the Scots had begun to discover that parliament was an instrument through which they could disagree with kings without necessarily taking to arms or flight. There were still risks; some critics found themselves in prison charged with offences not easy to refute before judges anxious to keep royal favour. Estates were sequestered or ruinous fines imposed. Nevertheless, more and more members of the nobility found the courage to speak out against legislation introduced by the Committee of the Articles and, finding safety in numbers, took a leaf out of the English book and refused to approve taxes until grievances were remedied. The king had sent them home and done without parliament, but some victories had been scored. Since 1653 Cromwell, Charles and James had in turn forbidden the General Assembly of the Kirk to meet. Robbed for thirty-five years at national level of the spiritual thunderings in which their fathers had indulged, Presbyterians with seats in parliament had been forced to find an outlet for their grievances in secular and material growling and grumbling from its benches. In 1689, the Scots as a whole were still far behind the English in appreciation of their parliament as a possible protection against tyranny or a means of promoting national or sectional interests. Enough, however, of the nobility and the lowland gentry were developing a taste for parliamentary debate, and an understanding of the part parliament might play in protecting and developing their own interests, to ensure that Scottish Whigs would make an effort to get as much for themselves out of the choice of monarchs as their English counterparts were getting.

The issue of human versus divine right was decided at a convention of the estates in Edinburgh. William's forces were all in England or in Holland. The only military forces in Scotland, other than the Highland clansmen, were the dragoons with which Graham of Claverhouse, Viscount Dundee, had hunted and harried the Covenanters. Dundee was for James and if he had concentrated his dragoons around Edinburgh and called in the clans, he could have awed Whigs into silence and waverers into James's camp, and divine right would probably have carried the day – at least until William could spare the time and the troops to bring Scotland into line by force. By taking himself instead to the clans in Perthshire he allowed the Cameronians from the south-western counties to march to Edinburgh and do the over-awing, threatening the vengeance of the God of Calvin on any weaklings who were tempted to cast a vote for the God of kings and popes. The arrival of veterans of William's continental war under the command of General Mackay put the matter beyond further doubt. The convention pronounced James to have forfeited the Scottish crown and offered it to William and Mary. All hope of the clansmen being able to overturn the decision ended some weeks later when Dundee was killed at Killiecrankie.

Scots got everything they wanted for their parliament and their Kirk from William. The Committee of the Articles was abolished and the autocratic rule of the Privy Council curbed by a parliament able, for the first time in its history, to become an independent force in the national life. William would have liked to put the Presbyterian and Episcopal churches on an equal footing in Scotland. He found it anomalous that a church with the same creed and system as that of which he was head in England should be denied even a lawful existence in his other kingdom of Scotland. He believed that to grant Episcopalians the right to practice their religion without dissimulation would be the quickest way to wean them from James. He was advised, however, that the Scots Presbyterians, who had given him the throne, could not be expected to distinguish between a bishop in Aberdeen and the Bishop of Rome and that if he wished peace in Scotland he must give the Kirk the sole supremacy its extremer adherents demanded.

Toleration was utterly rejected. John Knox's democratic church government was fully restored, even to the extent of depriving aristocratic landowners of their rights of patronage. Scots divines thundered again at God and the nation as they had done in the General Assembly before 1653. But, whatever standing it continued to enjoy with God, the General Assembly was no longer the one place in Scotland where men debated the nation's good. Through its synods, its presbyteries, its kirk sessions and congregations, the Kirk was in much closer touch with the people than parliament, with its very limited electorate, but in the hour when its denominational supremacy was restored the Kirk's power in the country was diminished. In gaining independence of the crown the members of parliament had also made themselves independent of the Kirk. For the first time since the Reformation they felt able to talk to crown and country outside it and without it; they could even see parliament protecting the Kirk. A new instrument had come into being through which the lay mind of the country – or at least that part of it that mattered – could express itself. The secular needs and material interests of the owners of land and other means of production could be debated and decided in parliament by the owners themselves without undue interference from the nation's spiritual advisers. Scotland had also had its Glorious Revolution. A new dimension had been added to Scottish politics, a new freedom and new possibilities gained by the propertied minority of the population.

It went to their heads, of course. Factions appeared and disappeared within and across the hazy demarcation lines of Whig and Tory as members tried to push advantages or pursue vendettas. In celebrating release from despotism, their reminders to King William that he should not rule without them were often irresponsible, and his ministers must have longed for some of the gags formerly in use. William had to prorogue the first session of his new parliament to escape the humiliation of being compelled by act of parliament to dismiss a capable and trusted minister who had incurred the voluble dislike of a large faction of members. His surrender to the Presbyterians over the toleration question avoided war in the country but did not make things easier for him in parliament. Episcopalians were confirmed in their Jacobite sympathies and eagerly joined with subversive intent in the parliamentary and popular indignation over the massacre of Glencoe and the failure of the Darien scheme described in the next chapter.

The thirteen years of William's reign had three important consequences in Scotland. As will be seen later, it convinced many Scots that their material prospects were now as hampered by having a king who ruled from London as their spiritual peace had been harried under Charles and James, and that sharing with England had better be ended if it could not embrace more than a head that wore two crowns. Secondly, the echoes of resulting rows in parliament were heard and listened to, as never before, by people on the land and in the towns who were becoming aware for the first time that words spoken and votes taken in parliament possibly could have as much effect on their lives and destinies as had decisions of the crown and debates in the Kirk. Lastly, members of the Scottish parliament began to realise that they now had the power, not only to bully the king of Scotland and his Scottish government, but to threaten the king of England and his English government. They saw that this power had possibilities. They had made a bargain with King William. It had been agreed that his sister-in-law Anne would succeed him in Scotland as well as in England. But it looked as if Anne would be childless. Parliament would have the power to bargain about her successor – to bargain with the government and parliament of England. It was an exciting thought, for the Whigs as well as the Jacobite Tories.

The thought also occurred to William. He was alive to the danger for England if the Scots should use the precedent of his own election to their throne to bargain whether its occupant after Anne should be other than sat on England's. 'Nothing can contribute more to the present and future peace, security and happiness of England and Scotland,' he said in a recommendation to his English parliament in 1702, 'than a firm and entire union between them.' He meant one crown and one parliament. Unhappily, it was on his deathbed that the words were spoken. All he could do was to bequeath the idea, with other problems, to Queen Anne.

The blunt fact is that the whole hundred years from 1603

neither the English nor the Scots were really aware of any benefits from the union of their crowns. They knew the crowns had
been worn on and taken off the same heads, with similar alarms
and excursions, marching and counter-marching, death and destruction, cheers and groans in both countries, but – unless they
were intimately concerned in the changes, or had carried pike and
musket across the border under Civil War command, or had
called down a Scots curse on a murdering English dragoon – they
had no reason to be interested in, much less grateful for, each
other's existence. Except for the brief period of Cromwell's rule,
they shared nothing whatever in common but the occupants of
their thrones, for even their sufferings at the hands of these had
different causes. England was richer because it farmed better and
because of its trade with its colonies and the East, which owed
nothing to the Scots. Scotland remained desperately poor agri-
culturally and was excluded from the overseas trade, although
the union could not in fairness be blamed for that. The English
felt under no obligation to ease the burden of their neighbours'
poverty and the Scots had nothing to bargain with. In all matters
of their national economies the two countries went their separate
ways, although in the last decade of the century the financial
genius of an emigrant Scot named William Paterson presented the
English with the new Bank of England and invented their national
debt.

For most of the century, with Stuart kings on both thrones,
English governments had no worries about Scotland becoming a
base for a foreign invasion of England. This was the solitary advantage England gained from uniting the crowns but it was not
one to which the population gave much thought. The union had
more effect on the Scots. Few and mostly harsh as their contacts
were with the English, some Englishness rubbed off on the
Scots. As a result, they awakened in the last years of the period
to the need for some semblance of a deliberative parliament, and
began to free themselves from the domination of the pulpit.

The clans of the Highlands had moved barely, if at all, out
of the Middle Ages. The Reformation had done much to persuade
the lowlanders to exchange the sword for the Word but, Kirk
government apart, the organisation of society, the methods of
work, the general outlook on human life and prospects were still

not far from feudal. Compared with the English as they had become by the last quarter of the seventeenth century, the lowland
Scots were an under-developed people in everything but raw
reasoning power. The Scottish lairds were aware, however, of how
much better off many English squires were in revenues and the
comforts of life, and were slowly coming round to the idea that it
might not be beneath the dignity of a gentleman to study other
ways of improving his income than by harrying his tenants or his
neighbours, or marrying a dowry. Roving Scots returned with
accounts of the wonders being wrought by ditching and draining
in water-logged areas of the south, and of the extra capital thus
obtained, which the English nobility and gentry were not above
investing in trade and industry, enriching themselves still further,
particularly from ventures in the American colonies and in the
companies trading with the east. It was observed too that the
English lords and squires used their Parliament for more than
changing their kings and exalting their church. They promoted
and passed laws which added to their wealth and that of the
traders and shipowners with whom they were in league. This was
something no Kirk Assembly could do. It made the case for a
parliament, for a secularly-oriented rather than a spiritually-
directed machinery of government, a concern for this life even
more than the next.

Men of power and influence in Scotland were beginning to
think they ought to copy the English and have an effective
parliament, with their own Scottish colonies and trading companies. Some were becoming bold enough to say that if Scotland
could not be richer on its own a closer union must be sought with
England. The important thing was to become rich, even if it meant
becoming more and more like the English. This kind of talk was
limited, of course, to a small section of the population, the majority
having no expectation of an improved lot in this world and no
reason to ape the English. It was anathema to Kirk stalwarts who
saw it simply as another machination of Satan to lure the nation
off the narrow path of Presbyterian self-righteousness and plunge
it in the bog of English episcopacy.

Intelligent Scots would no doubt have been acute enough to
observe the benefits of being English even if there had been no
union of the crowns. It was these two things, however – the im-

munity England had enjoyed from foreign attack from behind and the ambition of some Scots lairds to be as well-off as some English squires – which combined, when the question of succession to the two thrones next arose, to make possible the next phase of union – the union of the parliaments.

3 Any King but England's

In the spring of 1703, exactly one hundred years after James VI and I made his triumphal progress into England to unite the crowns, the Scots were in a bitterly angry mood. Before the summer was out they had served notice on the English that if the union were not quickly and generously amended in their favour they would tear it apart and have a monarch of their own, caring little whom so long as their crown sat on a different head from England's. In 1603 God and a handful of Englishmen had united the crowns and the Scots, all but one, had had no say in it. In 1703 the whole Scots nation was determined to separate them.

The mood was not new, but certain events had greatly exacerbated the bitterness and swelled the determination. First of these had been the notorious Massacre of Glencoe in 1692. A Highland village of Macdonalds had been wiped out by royal troops, to whom they had been giving hospitality, because their chief was six days late in taking the oath of loyalty to William of Orange. The treachery and cruelty of the incident, and the belief that the troops had acted on direct orders from the London-based foreigner king himself, roused the Scots to a national fury. The extent to which William bore any personal responsibility was far from clear, and there was undoubtedly Scots involvement in the affair at intermediate levels. Nevertheless it was against the king that the anger mounted. If he had not ordered the massacre, why did he not punish those who were responsible? William was forced to set up an inquiry by the Scottish parliament; he was found not guilty, and the inquiry condemned the barbarity of the troop commander, who fled the country and was outlawed. Popular disgust and anger remained unabated and, however unjustifiably, the outrage to humanity was passionately cited whenever and wherever the iniquities of union were discussed.

Even more maddening to the Scots, because it cost hundreds of them far more money than they could afford to lose, dashed all their hopes of entering the modern world and becoming a richer nation, and showed up their commercial inexperience and ineptitude, was the Darien disaster. We have already noted how Scots lords and lairds had begun to cast envious eyes on the profits of overseas trade which were filling the pockets of English nobles and squires and to talk of starting ventures of their own. In 1695 a number of them, inspired by William Paterson, the émigré Scot who had sold the idea of the Bank of England to the English government and who made a fortune out of organising London's water supply, set up the Scottish Africa and India Company to compete with the East India Company, which had held a monopoly of the English trade with the east since Elizabeth's time. The scheme generated a wave of wild excitement throughout Scotland. The national caution about easy money, born of centuries of having to look at every hard-won penny ten times before spending it, collapsed in a fever of patriotic belief that, given the opportunity, the Scots could be just as good at money-making as the English and that Scotland could no longer tolerate being denied a share of the warm sun of the east by English greed and jealousy. In a frenzy of enthusiasm and anticipation of the rewards to come, every bawbee that could be squeezed from meagre domestic economies was subscribed to the funds of the new company. A quarter of a million pounds, almost a third of the total cash circulation of the country, was contributed. This was less than the organisers considered adequate, but they had not been counting on Scottish investment alone. They knew there was money in England available for oriental ventures but legally debarred from them by the statutory monopoly of the East India Company. There was wealth in Hamburg too which they intended to tap, so they advertised for subscribers there and in London.

Their first mistake was badly to underestimate the power of the English organisation whose supremacy they were naively challenging. The East India Company had no difficulty in persuading the government in London to tell the Hamburg merchants in the name of King William that if they subscribed any money to William's Scottish subjects the whole trade in English cloth for Germany and eastern Europe which had hitherto passed through Hamburg would be switched to Bremen. It mattered nothing to the Hamburgers that William's English fist was being used to black his Scottish eye. They could afford to lose Scotland's trade through their port but not England's. The Scots returned from Hamburg empty-handed. It was almost as easy for the East India Company to lobby the English parliament into passing a law forbidding English subscriptions to the Scottish fund. The Scots had perforce to make do with the quarter million they had scraped out of their own pockets.

It was too little to allow them to build or buy an expensive fleet of ships for the sea-route round Africa to India and fill them with the kind of cargoes (most of which would have to be bought outside Scotland) that they must sell or exchange there to be able to bring back the tea, spices and treasures out of which their fortunes were to be made – all in fierce competition with the wealthy and wily English company which had shown it would stop at nothing in defence of its preserves. They thought of reviving the mediaeval land route from Europe to the east but were sensible enough to see it was hardly less expensive and much more hazardous. They could not let themselves be beaten, however. Scotland had to crash a way into wealth in the new century just ahead. If they could not go east, they would go west. They would do as Columbus had originally tried to do and get to the east by crossing the Atlantic. They were aware, of course, of what had stopped Columbus from reaching India – the huge land mass of the Americas – but they would take advantage of it. They decided, on Paterson's suggestion, to try to found a colony on the Isthmus of Darien at the narrowest point between the Atlantic and the Pacific. Cargoes brought by sea from Europe would be unloaded there, whisked across the narrow neck of land, and shipped again to India and China, the process being reversed for the return cargoes. They painted a wonderful picture for themselves of ships shuttling continuously across the Atlantic and the Pacific with a busy criss-cross of traffic on the isthmus and a new Scotland arising at the strategic centre of the modern world, a junction between old and new, east and west, and midway between the thriving English and French colonies to the north and the Spanish and Portuguese El Dorados to the south. It might have been a bold conception anticipating the Panama Canal but for one thing – none of them had ever been to Darien and all they knew was what they could glean by loosing their covetous imaginations around a dot on the map.

In 1698 three ships – one of which had William Paterson himself on board – set sail laden with traditional Scots bonnets, homemade serge cloths, huckabacks, stockings, bobwigs, periwigs, gridirons and the first batch of eager colonists. To do the Scots justice, they were not proposing to sell these unlikely wares to the Chinese, Malays and Indians. The purpose of this first expedition was to lay the foundations of the colony and give it a self-supporting start by trading initially with any Spanish and English colonists within reach. Unfortunately, there were more hard facts of international and commercial life which the organisers had overlooked or ignored. The isthmus of Darien had already been pre-empted by the King of Spain and when the Scots landed a Spanish force was sent to drive them out. They resisted successfully but the King of Spain invoked a treaty he had with William as King of England under which all trade within the Spanish dominions was reserved for Spaniards. The reservation dated, in fact, from the days of James I who, while endeavouring to marry his son Charles to the King of Spain's daughter, had accepted a line drawn through the Americas and down the ocean beyond which everything was Spanish and had forbidden English seamen to cross it. The ban had never been observed and in Charles II's time the seafaring populations of England and her American colonies had openly applauded the buccaneer exploits of their more daring countrymen in the islands and keys of the Spanish Main. The deliberate setting up of a colony on mainland Spanish territory was a newer and more serious challenge to Spanish authority, however, and William could not afford to take any risk of falling out with the Spaniards. Spain had been one of his allies in the war with France which had just been ended by the Treaty of Ryswick. Indeed, most of the fighting had taken place in the Spanish Netherlands. William knew that Louis XIV had only made peace to gather strength for another attempt to dominate Europe and also that he was determined next time to have Spain, with its territories in the Netherlands and Italy and its vast wealth overseas, on his side. Charles II of Spain had no heir and was not expected to live long. Claimants to the succession were Leopold, Archduke of Austria and Holy Roman Emperor; Louis XIV's own heir, the Grand Dauphin of France, and his sons; and a four years old Bavarian prince. The Grand Dauphin's claim would have been the best, because his mother had been the eldest daughter of Charles II's predecessor on the Spanish throne, had she not renounced her claim on marrying Louis XIV. Louis was not one to be deterred by such a legality and was intriguing to get the Spanish throne, if not for his own heir, for the Dauphin's younger son, Philip of Anjou. William was working hard to thwart this scheme or, if he could not prevent a French prince from sitting on the Spanish throne, to have it agreed by Louis that the Austrian claimant would have such a large share of the Spanish empire that the great French king's gains would be halved. The future of Europe hung on the outcome of the diplomacy in which William's ambassadors in Madrid, Paris and Vienna were engaged. The Scots could not have chosen a worse place and a worse moment, so far as their king was concerned, to make their bid for a larger share in the world's wealth. He issued a proclamation forbidding English colonists in America and the West Indies to have any truck with the invading Scots.

This third blow struck at their aspirations by their own king need not have doomed the Scots colonists if the organisers had had the foresight to send them out with any money. Spaniards could not trade with them under penalty of their king's displeasure but the English colonists cared little about offending King William if they could profit from their transgressions. There were also Dutch traders in Curacao who had no antipathy to Scots. The Scots found that nothing would grow in Darien and were riddled with fever. The English colonials and the Dutch would happily have supplied them with food and medicines if they had been able to pay for them. But nobody wanted their bonnets and wigs and gridirons and their pockets were empty, so the ships from Massachusetts and Curacao sailed away again, leaving them to die of malaria and starvation. Unaware of how the pioneers were faring, a second expedition crossed the Atlantic and found a few miserable survivors. The newcomers tried desperately to make a success of it but they were soon in no better case than the first contingent and by this time the Spaniards were back in strength. A handful of men struggled back to Scotland, leaving the bones of two thousand of their fellows behind in the Darien swamps, and their country's quarter of a million pounds and hopes of fortune vanished. Paterson was among the survivors but was seriously ill and for a time lost his reason.

Naturally enough, the Scots blamed this national disaster on the English and the union. In his capacity of king of England the king of Scotland had hamstrung them at every turn. Forgotten were the elements of sheer folly and commercial incompetence in the tragedy. The fact that all who had participated in the financing of the company were now so much poorer than before shot their anger through with real anguish. Nor was there anything in sight for most of them to alleviate the pain. In the period of the Darien disaster there was a succession of bad harvests due to appalling weather, which prevented the grain from ripening. The subsistence farmers had no reserves with which to buy food from abroad, so while their more adventurous compatriots were dying of starvation in Darien the folk who remained at home were being decimated by the same complaint. In some parishes the death-roll amounted to half of the inhabitants. Happily with the accession of Anne to the throne the weather had improved and the horrors of famine were lifted, but existence remained hand to mouth for landworkers and most of their lairds.

In England industry, agriculture, commerce were all expanding. 'The enterprise of trader and middleman was finding new markets for the products of the peasant's and craftsman's toil,' says G. M. Trevelyan of the beginning of Queen Anne's reign in his *English Social History*. 'Money made in trade was more and more frequently put into the land by improving landlords, who had won or enlarged their fortunes as mercantile investors. . . . A great interchange of agricultural products was going on between one district and another. . . . The Wiltshire and Cotswold uplands, that bred sheep for the western wool-clothiers, were a wonder to behold. . . . Men were everywhere building or enlarging farm-houses. . . . Fine country houses were rising. . . . Peace unbroken since the Civil War was multiplying the comforts of life. . . . Every county joined in the great national business of supplying London with food, coal or raw material. In return she sent to every county the finished goods of her own luxury trades, and the distant products of her foreign merchandise.'

The agricultural and industrial outlook of the Scots was as bleak as the land itself.

'Their country is that barren wilderness
Which Cain did first in banishment possess,'

wrote one of the very few Englishmen who had the hardihood to
pay a visit to Scotland in the opening years of the eighteenth
century. Only about a quarter of the country was cultivable. The
rest was rocky mountain or treeless moor, offering only rough
pasture in its accessible parts. Cultivation in the lowlands was
carried out on the lower slopes of hills because the flat land in
the valleys was undrained and waterlogged. The now fertile land
in the midlands and up the east coast was largely peat-bog. The
wasteful 'run-rig' system of small plots and ridges prevailed and
farm implements were antiquated and inadequate. Pasture lands
remained poor for lack of manure and little or nothing was done
to improve them, as in England, by the introduction of artificial
grasses. Agricultural production was generally at subsistence level,
landowners and tenants growing their own family needs in oats
for the staple food, barley for ale, flax for linen, and pease and
beans to vary the diet. A few head of cattle provided milk, butter
and cheese, some meat for the laird, and drew the clumsy plough.
Pigs and poultry were generally owned by lairds and potatoes were
grown only for their tables. Nine-tenths of the farms had no walls
or fences. Trees and hedges were discouraged so that there would
be no nesting for birds that might feed on the scarce grain. Everywhere but in the Highlands and along the Clyde, where there
were still some forests and woodlands, the land had a ragged, bare,
unfriendly aspect.

The only produce of the land in which there was trade were
cattle and sheep, skins of wild animals, salmon, and some timber
which was floated down the rivers from the Highlands. Lean,
stunted black cattle formed the largest export. Twenty to thirty
thousand head a year, from Galloway and the Highlands, crossed
the border for fattening on the richer English pastures. Beasts not
sold at the autumn cattle fairs were slaughtered to provide the
gentry with salt meat, or penned in dark byres and fed on straw
until the 'lifting' in spring, when the starved animals, too weak to
walk unaided, were carried back to the moor or hillside. Other
exports were live sheep from the border dales, wool and sheepskins;
cattle hides; skins of deer, goats, otters, rabbits and badgers;
salmon; and herring which, smoked or salted and barrelled, went

to France, the Low Countries, and the Baltic lands. Few lairds and no tenants accumulated capital by selling these relatively primitive goods, unchanged from those their forebears dealt in centuries earlier. Land was leased for no more than a year and tenants had no incentive to try to get more than a living out of their toil. The annual money incomes of landowners were around ten per cent of those of their English counterparts in the early 1700s. Fifty pounds a year was average, five hundred real wealth. Rents were paid at least half in kind. Tenants and their families lived in single rooms, lacking chimneys and windows and often un-separated from cattle at the other end. Lords and lairds had more accommodation, but few of the luxuries English peers and squires were enjoying. Their mansions of gaunt stone were without archi-tectural design or embellishment, flower gardens or lawns, carpets on the floors or pictures on the bare plaster of the walls. Bedrooms rarely knew the warmth of fires. Lockhart of Carnwath, a commoner who plays some part in this story, was rich by Scottish standards but he had inherited wealth made by his father and grandfather out of the practice of the law. The rent-rolls of grandees among the nobility – the Dukes of Queensbury, Hamilton, Atholl, Argyll – could reach four figures, but peers in the Scottish parliament were mostly poor, often plagued by creditors like the Earl of Mar, and all, including the richest, were eager to improve their incomes by holding government office or enjoying some other share in the spoils of royal patronage. Party strife was embittered by chagrin and envy and opposition majori-ties were difficult to secure when passions were not strongly roused and the government was ready to bribe to get its way. Scottish peers and commoners were not more venal than those at Westminster. Poverty gave them more excuse.

The towns were in little better shape than the country. The craft guilds – tailors, bonnet-makers, weavers, shoemakers, masons, woodworkers, blacksmiths, locksmiths, silversmiths – still made their wares only to order. The merchant guilds controlled all trade with the landward areas and abroad. Admission to the guilds was rigorously controlled by existing members, who also controlled membership of the burgh councils, who in turn con-trolled burgh representation in parliament. Industry and trade were therefore locally and nationally in the hands of self-perpetuating oligarchies, more concerned to keep them so than to promote development. Past practices stayed unaltered. Ports on the east coast traded with the Baltic, the Low Countries and France, the western ports with England, Ireland and France. Cargoes were mainly the hides, skins and fish mentioned above, plus some raw wool, some coal and lead, a very small quantity of woollen and a larger quantity of linen cloth. Influential landowners who raised sheep saw easier gain in supplying raw wool to the Baltic and the Low Countries than in supporting wool manufacture in Scotland, so they persuaded parliament to allow an export which had long been banned in England to the mutual advantage of landowners and manufacturers. The money brought in by export of cheap raw materials was spent on expensive foreign luxury goods in the limited quantities a small sector of the population could afford. Nothing was happening in Scotland to set in motion the processes of growth in agricultural and manufacturing production, and the domestic and overseas exchange of increasing quantities of good and services, which was distinguishing England's economy and producing surpluses for investment. On the contrary, Scottish overseas trade was declining. Dutch fishermen were capturing traditional Scottish markets on the continent with herring which they were impudently catching in increasing volume in Scottish waters. The ports on the Fife coast, whose prosperity had justified James VI and I's lyrical description of the county as 'a beggar's mantle fringed with gold', were dismissed by Fletcher of Saltoun at the turn of the century as 'little better than so many heaps of ruins'. The population of Glasgow, regarded as Scotland's commercial capital although it was still little more than an attractive village, had declined during the previous decade to 12 500 while that of Bristol had risen to 30 000. Glasgow had thrived when its sea-captains and merchants had access under Cromwell to the sugar, tobacco, mahogany and oranges of the West Indies and the American colonies. When Charles II's Navigation Act of 1660 reserved all legitimate trade once again for Bristol and other English ports, Glasgow had to be content with such cargoes as could run the gauntlet of the English navy. No more than fifteen ships with a total tonnage of under 1 200 tons were trading in and out of the Clyde with all markets. It was this state of affairs the Scots had hoped to remedy by the Darien venture.

Efforts had been made to improve the economy. In retaliation

for the abolition of Cromwell's free trade the Scottish parliament
had clapped heavy duties on the import of English cloth, hats,
stockings and gloves, and had set up a Council of Trade to promote
manufactures and commerce. Hopeful of repeating the benefits
England had reaped from Huguenot immigration, the Council
offered advantageous terms to foreign artisans to settle in Scotland
and make the English articles the duties were excluding. Few
came, the English found other markets, and fewer Scots ladies
wore stockings on their legs and gloves on their hands. An act of
1681 banned English and continental gold and silver thread, laces
and buttons, silk, linen, cambric, lawn, calico and damask, and in
1686 it was enacted that corpses could be buried only in 'Made in
Scotland' winding sheets – all to force the Scots to find the will,
the skills, and the capital to go into industry. These were not
wholly lacking. Joint stock companies had become a rage in
England and over fifty were started in Scotland, not to make the
finer forbidden things, but to weave linen, silk, sail-cloth and ropes,
make soap, gunpowder, pottery and paper, refine sugar and found
iron. Inducements were offered. Woollen mills were started in
East Lothian on a guarantee that no taxes would be levied on
anything they handled, including the alcoholic liquors drunk by
their employees. In 1695 a Bank of Scotland was established with
a capital of £10 000.

Nothing was very successful, however. The new goods the Scots
were making were neither of the type nor the quality to be ex-
portable except to markets less sophisticated than their own. Bans
on imports were not enforced because those who could afford the
forbidden articles were unwilling to do without them and nobody
in Scotland was qualified to make them. Capital was difficult to
raise because burghers with money would not diversify their own
activities or help others to start new trades. Nobles and lairds
were the chief providers of capital for the new ventures but the
number with money to risk was not large and they took a very
bad knock in the failure of the Darien scheme before seeing any
encouraging return from their investments in the fifty companies
mentioned.

Scots at the beginning of the eighteenth century were much
in the position and mood of the peoples of the under-developed
countries of the second half of the twentieth century. They were
the 'have-nots', and the prosperous English were the 'haves'. They

had not been conquered, colonised, or exploited, but they felt they had been annexed by the union of the crowns and held back and held down through that annexation, in ways which only the more travelled and educated among them could define and discuss, but which all classes outside the Highlands had come to think of as creating a barrier between them and that better life which they were told the English enjoyed – a barrier that had to be removed.

Other things had happened to enrage the Scots against the one-sided operation of the union. In 1701 the English parliament decided that something had to be done to secure the succession to the throne. William and Mary were childless and the longest-surviving of sister Anne's seventeen children had died the year before at the age of nine. They passed an Act of Settlement vesting the succession after the deaths of William and Anne in the Protestant House of Hanover, whose Dowager-Electress Sophia was a grand-daughter of James I. This was done without any consultation whatever with the Scots parliament. It was blandly assumed by all concerned in London that anybody on whom they conferred the English crown would automatically put on the crown of Scotland. To have simply forgotten about Scotland would have been insult enough. They had, however, impudently included references to Scotland in a series of resolutions embodied in the act, one of which forbade the wearer of the crown to leave England, *Scotland* or Ireland without the *English* parliament's consent. The Scots were well aware that their governors took their orders from London but these had at least come in the past in the name of a monarch they had accepted as their own. Now the English, with all the deliberation of parliamentary process and debate in two Houses, had had the arrogance to assume the right to put a line of German princelings over them, without so much as a by-your-leave, and to tell their appointee that he would need their permission to leave Scotland if he ever set foot in it. This was behaving as if Scotland were as much an English possession as Ireland or Wales or one of the American colonies. At one moment the English commanded the rest of the world to treat them as rank outsiders with no claim to any kinship or connection, and at the next swept them under the family table as if they were no more than domestic curs. Since this was what union had come to mean the sooner it was ended the better.

When William died and Anne came to the double throne in 1701, the utter indifference of London to Scottish institutions and feelings was further demonstrated. Three days after her accession Anne appeared before the English parliament and in thanking the peers and commons for their addresses of loyalty assured them that 'she knew her heart to be entirely English'. At her coronation commemorative medals were tossed in handfuls among the assembled grandees and representatives of foreign countries with the words 'Entirely English' engraved on them around her head. All that was thought necessary to mark her assumption of the Scottish crown was a meeting of the Scottish Privy Council. It is not recorded whether the members awarded themselves any of the 'Entirely English' medals.

None of Anne's predecessors on the two thrones had shown any warmth towards their Scottish subjects. They had seen them as a problem they could well have done without. At no previous time, however, had it been more desirable that the English and the Scots should be ruled by a monarch inspiring trust and affection on both sides of the border. Anne was not equipped to be such a ruler. Her health was poor, her spirits often low from recurrent bouts of gout and dropsy, and the responsibilities of her position always weighed heavily on her slow-working mind. She was devoid of any kind of sparkle in her public appearances and completely tongue-tied if required to converse with strangers. Consequently she led as retired a life as possible and inspired no affection outside the small circle of her household. She had paid one visit to Scotland, in 1681 at sixteen years of age when her father, then Duke of York, was appointed by Charles II to be Lord High Commissioner in his other kingdom and preside over its Parliament. She found no reason on that occasion to like Scotland or the Scots. Her strongest interests throughout her life were the Church of England and her food, and Scotland was not the place to afford her satisfaction in either of them. The divines of the Kirk made her shudder, and on their side they could see little difference between her enthusiasm for the English church in its most hierarchical and ritualistic manifestations and the Church of Rome to which her father so frighteningly belonged. She could see nothing attractive or sympathetic in the Presbyterians she met, and the Scots Episcopalians had been too preoccupied with steering a middle course between Popery and Presbyterianism to be concerned about her religious loneliness in Edinburgh. Scots food was coarse and she could get none of the titbits to which she was addicted. She was not without humane feeling for her fellow-men and women, and she had her own tortuous powers of reasoning on matters of state, but even now as Queen of Scotland she could not overcome the antipathy to Scots she had developed twenty years before.

Her English heart disliked more about the Scots than their religion and their food. As Queen of England, she was very conscious of the menace, to her growing interests overseas, of the ambition of Louis XIV to be master of Europe and arbiter of its relationships with the rest of the world. England could not allow the balance of power in Europe to be swung in France's favour. That was why her brother-in-law William had fought so hard against the French. It was why – Louis having succeeded in setting his grandson, Philip, on the Spanish throne – she was about to send Marlborough to fight them again. Most Scots were indifferent to the menace of Louis; many of them made no secret that they would rather see the French dominate the world than the English. There was a danger that their present discontents might encourage Louis to believe he could find a base in Scotland from which to overthrow her rule in England or at least compel her to leave him alone in Europe. This danger would have been worry enough for a new sovereign as nervous and conscientious as Anne. The headache was intensified, however, by the complications of her own succession question, already pressing upon her although her reign was measurable only in months. Anne's great sorrow and tragedy was that she had no children. She was only thirty-six but had no hope of an heir of her body. Her twenty years of marriage to Prince George of Denmark had produced seventeen infant mortalities. For nine years there had been a possibility that the Duke of Gloucester might survive to obviate a succession problem, but, as has been mentioned, he died in 1698, three years before she reached the throne. By the Act of Settlement, passed on the day before William died, the English parliament had selected Sophia of Hanover to follow her in England. Sophia was seventy-one years old, but many times livelier than Anne herself. She was endowed, moreover, with a healthy son. The other claimant was Anne's thirteen years old half-brother, James, whose birth in 1688 had helped to precipitate the Glorious Revolution and bring William and Mary and Anne to the throne, and whose recognition by Louis XIV as the rightful king was another factor in forcing England to go to war with him again. Anne would have preferred her half-brother, but she was sufficiently logical to acknowledge that, if parliament had the right to give her a place in the succession when deposing her father, its right to select her own successor should be equally respected. Now the tiresome possibility was arising that the Scots might not adhere to the decision of the English parliament and take Sophia for their queen – for no better reason than that they had a parliament of their own and it had not been consulted. Indeed, in their pique they might be more disposed to welcome French troops; some might even be prepared to invite them over and to bring her half-brother with them.

Her immediate worry on assuming the throne, however, was how to reconcile her wish to have only High Churchmen and Tories as her English ministers with their marked disapproval of going to war with France. She loved and venerated the bishops and archbishops of the Church of England and all the spiritual and material splendours attending them, saw the powers of darkness at work in anything which questioned their right to speak for God in everything spiritual and temporal, and consequently had an almost pathological aversion to religious dissent. Those who shared her emotions about the church tended to be Tories in politics, so it was natural that she should feel most comfortable in the company of Tories and wish to have them as confidants and advisers and the executors of her policies. Unhappily, the cast of mind which brought them together with her in religion was separating them from her in matters of statecraft. The Tories were the lineal and spiritual descendants of the Cavaliers. Their fathers and grandfathers had fought for Charles in the Civil War and had suffered in consequence. Their families had looked to the Restoration to give them back everything they had lost. They had received a king, their church had become supreme again, expropriated lands were returned, and they enjoyed once more the powers and privileges of inherited rank and wealth. They had also looked to the Restoration to destroy their enemies; but in this they were disappointed for they survived in a new guise as the members of the Whig party.

The Whigs were compounded of four elements. First came

landowners. Some wealthy landowning families had been Parliamentarians, had retained their possessions under Cromwell, and had been forgiven by Charles under the influence of Clarendon's moderation and his own good-nature. Others had bought their way into the landed gentry at the expense of Royalists who had been forced to sell land to pay fines imposed on them by Cromwell. Confiscated royalist lands had been re-confiscated at the Restoration, but purchasers of land had been allowed to keep their purchases. Hated by ex-Royalists thirsting for some kind of revenge, the members of all such families banded together in their own protective interest as Whigs. Next came all whose form of Protestant religious belief would not allow them to join in the worship of the Church of England – the dissenters. Only communicants of the established church could hold office under the crown or be admitted to Oxford and Cambridge Universities. The clergy of the church and their fervent Tory supporters strenuously opposed any concessions to dissenters. Members of Protestant dissenting sects looked to the Whigs for relief, and the Whigs, by conviction or political interest, became the party of religious toleration. This brought in a third group – the freethinkers, rationalists and latitudinarians to be found throughout educated society in consequence of the interest in science and philosophy promoted by Newton, Locke and others. The fourth group belonged to the rapidly growing London business community, whose needs and interests as financiers and foreign traders made little appeal to insular, rusticating Tory clerics and squires.

Nothing in England's purely domestic politics could ever have induced Anne to entrust any part in her government to Whigs. They were creating or accepting changes in the social structure, the economy, the intellectual and spiritual frames of reference of the country, which the church and its more rabid Tory supporters were stubbornly resisting. The Whigs were welcoming possibilities of development offered by a new century. Church and Tories were determined to preserve unaltered the privileges they had salvaged from the last one, and Anne would have stood unquestioningly with them – had it not been for Louis XIV's imperialist ambitions and his recognition of her brother as King of England by divine right of birth. Whigs had no hesitation about answering Louis with a declaration of war. As the party of a new democracy they had doubly finished with the divine rights of kings – when they had first put William and Mary on the throne and later voted for the Electress of Hanover as Anne's successor. As religious tolerationists they abominated Louis for his cruel persecution of the Huguenots. As bankers and traders they could not permit France to gain control of Spain and world commerce. Tories were not so united. As members of the Church of England they had accepted William and Mary in preference to James and the Church of Rome. They had thought it advisable for the same reason to settle the succession on the House of Hanover. But many of them had not wholly abandoned divine right and cherished a hope that, when the time came, Anne's half-brother would be willing to accept the Church of England for the sake of the crown and make it possible for their party to take back its commitment to Hanover. They were finding it difficult, therefore, to make war on Louis because he preferred God's choice of a king for England to parliament's. Moreover, war demanded an army. War against Louis demanded a very large, well-trained, professional army, which was anathema to Tory squires for two reasons: taxation for its maintenance would traditionally fall more heavily on owners of land than on business men, who could hope to reap more benefits from the war than landowners could; also they remembered how Cromwell had used a well-trained professional army to despoil their fathers' England and disestablish her church, and they feared a possible recurrence if a similar weapon were placed in the hands of dissenter-loving Whigs. England's army, they argued, should be no more than a militia, raised when the defence of the country called for it and officered by reliable amateurs and gentlemen like themselves. There was nothing in the situation, as they saw it, necessitating war. Their England was not being threatened by Louis' acquisition of Spain.

Anne's predicament in the choice of a ministry would have been extreme if all Tories had been of this mind. Her closest confidant was Sarah Churchill, wife of the Earl of Marlborough, a Tory whose ambition, genius as a soldier, and conception of the role England must play in Europe and the world had combined to convince him that Louis must be frustrated. Pressed by the Marlboroughs, Anne was ready to go to war if she could do it without surrendering herself to a Whig ministry. Fortunately, other Tories besides Marlborough were outgrowing the party's prejudices. Division in the party corresponded to a division in the church. Anglican laymen in the cities and towns, in the secular professions, and in the army, were more liberal in their outlook than High Church clergy and country squires. Religious convictions and social connection kept them in the Tory party, but they did not ostracise all dissenters or consider they must stay forever deprived of higher education and office; they did not regard hunting, shooting and fishing as the only permissible interests of gentlemen; and they were prepared to agree that England might have need of wealth made outside the shires. It was chiefly this last divergence from the High Church section that disposed moderate Tories to see a case for going to war with Louis. With their help Marlborough found a way out of Anne's dilemma. He wanted war with Louis, but he was unwilling to start it unless he could be sure that parliament would stand firmly behind him and that money would be forthcoming to hold a continental allegiance together and secure him troops and supplies for a lengthy campaign. Whether Anne liked it or not, the war ministry would have to be predominantly Whig. Only Whigs could be trusted to see a long and expensive war through to a successful end. But Whigs alone could not do it. The majority in the Lords was Whig, in the Commons Tory. The Tory Commons would have the voting of the money supplies. A combination of Whigs and moderate Tories would have to be procured in the ministry to control both Houses. A man of real financial ability and probity would be needed at the helm. He proposed to Anne that her chief minister should be his own closest friend, the moderate Tory, Sidney, Lord Godolphin.

Marlborough and Godolphin had been friends from their early days at the court of Charles II. Godolphin's only son, Francis, had married the Churchills' eldest daughter, Harriet. Godolphin was a very experienced politician. A Cornishman, he had entered Charles II's household at an early age and had risen to be Baron Godolphin, head of the treasury, and close adviser to Charles, who said of him that 'he was never in the way and never out of the way'. He opposed James of York's efforts to give a more pro-Catholic turn to Charles's policies; but when James came to the throne he continued in ministerial office, went to mass with the king, and was entrusted with some of his most confidential dealings with Louis XIV. Remaining with James until it was certain the crown was lost, he nevertheless contrived to be one of the members of the House of Lords who went to treat with William at Hungerford. He controlled William's finances until he had to resign in 1696, because of accusations, which he denied, that he had been intriguing, like other Tories, with the exile court at St Germains. Four years later he was back because William needed a Tory minister, only to be out again in a year when the swing of the parliamentary pendulum brought back Whigs. He had been out of office when William died. Godolphin had undoubted financial experience and ability. He was acceptable to the moderate Tories and respected by the Whigs. Neither his history nor his person rendered him displeasing to Anne. High Tories distrusted him for being willing to co-operate with Whigs and for favouring war with Louis. This was distressing to Anne since he would not bring her nearer to her friends in the church. But he was the intimate associate of her other friends, the Marlboroughs, and thankfully he was not a Whig. She appointed him Lord High Treasurer.

Godolphin was not a great statesman, not even a very strong character. He was frequently timid in his approach to problems and could be discouraged. Sarah Churchill easily dominated him. But with Marlborough to beckon him on, and Sarah to push from behind, he nerved himself to accomplish most of what Marlborough expected of him. The hours he could spare were spent at the gaming table or in crossing Arab steeds with English horses to breed winners at Newmarket. One thing he felt no call to give his time to when he stepped into office was Scotland. He had no knowledge of or interest in it. Apart from his having many other preoccupations, it fell barely within his province as chief minister in the English administration. The queen had Scottish ministers to advise her on its problems. No doubt he saw these as small compared with his own. If he had to be involved in them, he would hear about them soon enough.

Neither of the English parties was much concerned about Scotland when Anne came to the throne. Once William was securely in the saddle the Whigs had given it little thought. Presbyterians had put him there, and, Presbyterians being dissenters in the eyes of Englishmen, they were regarded by Whigs as members of their own party or the nearest Scottish equivalent to it. William's Scots ministers had nearly all been accepted as

Whigs by their London colleagues. Anne appointed as her Lord High Commissioner to Scotland the Duke of Queensbury, who had been last holder of the office under William. The Whig members of Godolphin's new ministry had complete confidence in him. Godolphin liked him and approved his political skill. The High Tories hated Scots for being Presbyterians and had not forgotten how they had sold their revered King Charles the Martyr to Cromwell. Their only interest in the country was in speculating how many Highland chiefs and their clansmen would rise for James III if the French should help the boy to land there – and whether, if the French did, they could safely invite the tartan horde to use their claymores on English dissenters as effectively as they hoped they would use them on the Scottish Presbyterians.

There were three political parties in Scotland: supporters, like Queensbury, of the queen's government, who were willing to swallow English disregard of their country's independent status and accept the Hanover succession; a Country Party led by the Duke of Hamilton, whose members writhed at the injuries inflicted on Scots under William (and which looked like being continued under Anne) and were hot for re-asserting independence of a London government; and the Jacobites, who were all for rejecting a queen from Hanover and as soon as possible crowning the boy at St Germains. Queensberry's government party were not averse to England's going to war again with France; the Jacobites were praying the English would lose; the Country Party were too busy nursing their own grievances to care about England and France – but astute politicians among them were beginning to consider whether England's war might not be turned to Scotland's advantage. When Anne was forced to think about Scotland, which was not more often than she could help, she was galled that her only friends there appeared to be Presbyterians and Whigs.

There was a requirement on the statute book that the Scots parliament should assemble within twenty days of William's death and be dissolved within six months to allow for a general election. The members made little protest when they were not summoned to meet before the expiration of the twenty days, because William had died early in March and the weather in Scotland in that month had damped political ardours, but when this statutory requirement was not complied with there was a general expectation that an election would be held and that it would be a new parliament which would meet as the first of the reign. The Scots were looking forward to this election because they were determined to throw out the government that took orders from an 'entirely English' queen advised by an English ministry. The Duke of Queensberry was as determined that the government should remain and advised Anne to forget about an election and summon the old parliament. Ten days before it met more fuel was added to the fire. England had gone to war with France. Without waiting to give the Scots parliament a say, the Scots Privy Council hastened to obey its orders from London and threw Scotland in on the English side. This was more than most Scots were prepared to take.

The Scots parliament met in a single chamber, lords and commons together. When it assembled in June 1702, before the Duke of Queensberry could declare it in session, the Duke of Hamilton rose and denounced the meeting as illegal. When Queensberry refused to accept his protest he walked out and was followed by some eighty members in a preconcerted procession in order of rank. The Edinburgh mob whooped and cheered as the dissidents marched through them to a tavern, where they sat down to a banquet at which they swore to boycott parliament until an election returned it to legality. The other members, about one hundred and twenty, carried on. In her 'entirely English' speech in the London parliament Queen Anne had expressed the hope that her two parliaments would consider the possibility of a closer union of her two peoples. The rump of the Scots parliament dutifully approved a government motion that the queen should appoint representatives of their country to discuss the matter, on condition that Presbyterianism should be preserved as the national religion and that the terms of any agreement reached be referred back to parliament. Even they baulked, however, at the government's wish to commit Scotland to England's chosen House of Hanover. They insisted that the national grievances against England should be remedied first, and when Lord Marchmont, the Chancellor, tried to introduce an act under which all members of parliament, office holders and ministers of the Kirk would have been required to forswear support of the claim of Anne's exiled Catholic brother James to the crown, they turned it down, staunch

Presbyterians though most of them were, by fifty-seven votes to fifty-three. The majority was a warning to England that Scotland was keeping its options open.

In this atmosphere of gathering tension representatives of the two countries, picked by the queen, met in London to discuss her suggestion of closer union. All the English were concerned about was to tie Scotland firmly to England and the Hanover succession. They proposed that, in addition to one king in London, there should be a single parliament, also in London. The Scots, selected for their expected tameness, indicated willingness at a price – complete freedom of trade with England and the colonies. When the English said no, they stood their ground. The Archbishop of York, one of the English negotiators, demanded that the Scots give up the Kirk. After three months of stonewalling on both sides the English suddenly gave in. The Scots could have their free trade. Immediately England was in a ferment. All the mercantile interests violently repudiated the trade proposal. The High Churchmen backed the Archbishop of York, refusing to sit in any parliament which included Presbyterians and recognised the Scottish Kirk. The English government got cold feet and when the next meeting of the negotiators was held the English side failed to field a quorum and Queen Anne adjourned the meetings indefinitely. England heaved a sigh of relief and the Scots spat venomously. In the spring of 1703 they got the election they had been waiting for.

The chief opponents in the election and the new parliament were the Dukes of Queensberry and Hamilton. Queensberry as Lord High Commissioner carried out the functions and exercised the authority of the crown in Scotland, much as governors-general represent and act for the queen today in Commonwealth countries of which she is the Head. He also presided over the single-chamber parliament. Monarchy was not detached from party politics, however, and the Commissioner was expected to secure that the actions of the Scottish ministers of the crown conformed as far as possible to the policies of the English ministers of the crown, which were generally congenial to the monarch who appointed and dismissed them, more or less at will. An able Commissioner of strong personality was the most powerful man in Scotland. Queensberry had the ability and the personality. The question was whether he would keep his power over the new parliament or lose it to Hamilton, leader of the Country Party, the largest group returned by the election. He would continue to hold office, as would the Scottish ministers, so long as the queen and her English ministers had confidence in them, but could he continue to hold parliament and the country to the wishes of the queen and the English ministers against the rebellious mood which the election had mandated Hamilton to voice?

Public opinion regarded the dukes as well-matched. They both bore the respected family name of Douglas and the Christian name of James. Hamilton traced his descent through a more imposing branch of the Douglas tree, had royal blood in his veins through the marriage of one of his ancestors to a sister of King James III of Scotland, and was the fourth duke of his line. Queensberry was only the second of his. Over the last thirty years the two families had vied with one another for position and power in Scotland. Both had been king's men in the Civil War and suffered in consequence. The sequestration of the Hamilton estates by Cromwell had forced the family into heavy debts. Queensberry's grandfather, the second earl of the name, had been so severely fined, first by the anti-royalist Scottish parliament and later by Cromwell, that he had been reduced nearly to penury. Both dukes' fathers set themselves to recover the family fortunes. Hamilton's mother had succeeded to the ducal title in her own right as daughter of the previous holder and had married another Douglas, the Earl of Selkirk. When the estates were returned after the Restoration, Selkirk restored the finances. His wife's petition to Charles II to create him Duke of Hamilton was granted and he entered the Scottish parliament in 1661 eager to attain the place in public affairs to which he felt his name and rank entitled him. Queensberry's father started later. He was too poor to be given a proper education for the heir to an earldom but he had ability and ambition. Within seven years of the Restoration he had worked his way up through minor offices to a seat on the Scottish Privy Council. After he succeeded to the family estates in 1671 economy and good management brought him some prosperity, and by the end of that decade, nearly twenty years behind Hamilton, he was ready to make a serious attempt on the heights of power.

Charles II's reign was not a happy one for Hamilton senior.

He made a mark in the Scottish parliament as a speaker in the Presbyterian interest and managed at first to be on good terms with the Duke of Lauderdale, Charles's Secretary for Scottish Affairs, whose favour was essential for any Scot anxious to succeed. Trouble arose between them when Lauderdale tried to get Charles out of some of his financial difficulties by imposing a heavier tax on Scottish landowners. They pressed Hamilton to lead their revolt in parliament. Lauderdale countered by offering to let Hamilton run Scotland in his stead if he would support the tax. Hamilton at first refused, then accepted and voted for the tax. To his chagrin, however, the unscrupulous Lauderdale made no move to implement his promise. Some time later, when Lauderdale asked the Scottish parliament to vote Charles still more money, Hamilton moved that no supplies should be forthcoming until the nation's grievances had been debated and remedied. Lauderdale hastily prorogued parliament and Hamilton was summoned to London. To his astonishment, the king was friendly. But when he returned to Scotland he found parliament had been dissolved and he was soon after dismissed from the Privy Council. Three times in ensuing years he led deputations to London to protest against Lauderdale's callous behaviour to the Covenanters but the king refused to see him. He had one solace in Charles's lifetime. When an act was moved to secure James, Duke of York, in the succession to the Scottish throne, Hamilton spoke so warmly in support that little opposition was voiced and as a reward the king, on James's recommendation, allowed him to fill the vacancy in the Knighthood of the Garter created by Lauderdale's death in 1682.

Queensberry senior, on the other hand, fared very well under Charles II. In 1680, thanks to influence with Chancellor Lord Rothes, he was made Lord Justice General. Two years later he was a marquess and within months was appointed, first Lord High Treasurer, then Constable and Governor of Edinburgh Castle, two of the most important offices in the kingdom. In another two years he was a duke. His rise had been meteoric, far outstripping Hamilton's.

When James succeeded Charles in 1685 the tide of fortune changed for both the fathers. Hamilton senior was reinstated to the Privy Council and in short sequence was appointed a commissioner of the treasury, an extraordinary lord of session, and a member of the English Privy Council, a remarkable series of favours from a would-be absolute Catholic king to a subject who in the previous reign had earned a reputation as a champion of Presbyterianism and resistance to the demands of the crown. He had had the good fortune – or the good sense – to give James his timely support. Queensberry *père* retained the offices he had held under Charles and in addition was James's first Scottish Commissioner, presiding over a parliament which meekly surrendered the proceeds of excise to the crown for ever, conferred the land tax on James for life, and extended the punishment of death to all who attended field conventicles, preached at house conventicles, or defended the National Covenant in speech or writing. He made the mistake, however, of informing James that, while he was ready to go to any lengths in supporting the royal power and persecuting Presbyterians, he could not assist in overturning the established Protestant religion. Consequently, when he had given his master all he immediately wanted from parliament, he was dismissed from all his offices and ordered to remain in Edinburgh until his treasury accounts had been examined. The Hamilton father was on the way up; but not as fast as the Queensberry father had gone down.

The sons now enter the story. Although Charles II had no time for Hamilton *père*, he took a liking to Hamilton *fils*. When Philip, Duc d'Anjou, was born in 1683, Charles selected Hamilton's son and heir, the twenty-five years old Earl of Arran, as an ambassador-extraordinary to convey his congratulations to Louis XIV on the birth of a second grandson. Arran stayed on happily at the French court until Charles's death when Louis sent him back to London with a recommendation to James which resulted in his appointment as gentleman of the royal bedchamber and master of the wardrobe, a post of some distinction and influence for one so young. The Hamiltons, father and son, were benefiting together under James, the son doing better than the father. Queensberry *fils* had not been left out, however. Before his father's dismissal, he had, at the age of twenty-two and a year after Arran's ambassadorial appointment, been made a Scottish Privy Councillor and second-in-command of Viscount Dundee's regiment of Covenanter-hunting horse, anticipating by a year his father's declaration of willingness to harry all Presbyterians.

Through him the Queensberrys still had a foot on the ladder, although the father had fallen badly.

When William and Mary came over from Holland and ousted James, the two fathers and the two sons performed a curious quadrille. The elder Queensberry, in spite of being so ignominiously dismissed and dishonoured by James, remained quietly faithful to his king until the latter fled to France and the convention of the estates declared the throne vacant. He then cast a discreet vote for William and Mary. It took them four years, in which he did not attempt to return to public life, to acknowledge the sacrifice he had made under James for the Protestant religion. They gave him a sinecure post as an extraordinary lord of session. He died two years later, just when his son may have found the ducal coronet and robes a welcome addition to the honours William and Mary were bestowing on him. The Jacobite George Lockhart of Carnwath contemptuously describes young Queensberry as 'the first Scotsman that deserted over to Prince William and from thence acquired the epithet (amongst honest men) of Proto-Rebel'. He was certainly well to the fore among those who hastened to William after his landing at Torbay in November 1688. William was pleased to have the adherence of the son of James's former chief minister in Scotland and himself so recently a leading harrier of the Covenanters. It was evidence that ambitious Scots, whatever brand of Protestantism they professed, were seeing him as the arbiter of their fortunes, and he was willing to encourage them. He appointed Queensberry junior to be colonel of the horse guards in Scotland, a member of his Scottish Privy Council, and a gentleman of his bedchamber. In 1692 he was made a commissioner of the treasury and a year later was elevated to his father's former office of Lord High Treasurer. All that the father had lost under the old dispensation, the son was retrieving under the new. Perhaps the older man was reconciled to leaving the power to struggle to a son who was evidently well qualified for it.

In the case of the Hamiltons, it was on the father that William and Mary smiled; the son was subjected to imprisonment and humiliation. While he had been accepting favours from James and watching his son making his way at that king's court, Hamilton senior had not wholly put away the Presbyterian and constitutionalist sympathies which he had evinced under

c

Charles. He was prepared for a change of allegiance when it should be advantageous. Consequently, when the critical moment came, he was closely behind young Queensberry in the race to be the first Scot to stand by the side of William and Mary. He called a meeting of all the Scots then in London and with their support framed an address requesting William to wrest the Scottish crown from James and summon a convention of the estates to regularise his position. At the convention which met in Edinburgh in March 1689 Hamilton was elected to the chair and duly proclaimed William and Mary as joint sovereigns. The convention then became a parliament and the grateful sovereigns chose Hamilton as the first Lord High Commissioner of their reign. He had reached the top of the ladder at last. He was re-appointed to the Commissionership in 1693 and died in 1694. Hamilton *fils*, like Queensberry *père*, had been slower to abandon James. He was far from the last to bow the knee to William but he made his obeisance with the declaration, extraordinary in the circumstances, that he was doing so at the command of his master, meaning James. This was regarded by William as an impertinence and he sent him to the Tower. He was brought to trial, but his judge found that the formalities had not been properly complied with and adjourned the trial. Shortly afterwards he was released. He was not forgiven, however. In spite of his father's success with William, he was again arrested, this time on suspicion of corresponding with the king's enemies in France, and languished for a year in the Tower before being released on bail. He was allowed to retire to Scotland where the apparently quiet and inoffensive life he led was interrupted by the issue of a warrant charging him with conspiracy against the realm. This charge was no more pressed than the others. It was mysteriously withdrawn without trial. Whether he was innocent and persecuted by enemies, or guilty and protected by his father, has never been decided. When Hamilton senior died in 1694 the estates and title reverted to his wife, the grant which Charles II made to him at her request having been for life only. Once again she petitioned, this time that she be allowed to resign her lands and title irrevocably in favour of her ill-used son. To everybody's surprise William granted the petition in 1698.

Queensberry added the Keepership of the Privy Seal to his other distinctions and in 1700 achieved the peak of his ambition.

King William chose him to be Commissioner in the parliament he unwillingly summoned to debate the situation arising from the Darien disaster. It was the most difficult parliament any Commissioner had faced. Never had so many members been so united in execration of the rule from London which the Commissioner represented. In all the debates the voice that spoke out most effectively in denunciation and demand was Hamilton's. In one session – his first in parliament – he rose from the unsavoury semi-obscurity in which he had languished to be hailed by an angry people as their heaven-sent spokesman. The leadership for which dissident Scots had looked to his father and only fitfully received they were now unexpectedly offered by the son and they hastened to give it welcome and support. For the first time the two dukes met in direct confrontation – Queensberry, thirty-eight, the complete 'establishment man' of his day, upholding the Protestant succession and rule from London because he was sure these were in the best interests of Scotland and himself, skilled courtier and parliamentarian, accustomed to position and power and determined to keep them, not unsympathetic to the griefs and grievances of his countrymen but unable to do anything to alleviate them because he could not see how without disturbing the system of government and economy which his masters in London insisted he must maintain; Hamilton, fortytwo, a man with a deep grudge against an establishment which had subjected him to prison and social ostracism, losing him years in which he ought to have been climbing high, bitterly jealous of Queensberry's success, raw to the intricacies of parliamentary manoeuvre, but endowed with a passionate eloquence and a haughty aggressive manner which endeared him immediately to those who found in Queensberry's smooth style of speech another evidence of how far he had sold himself to the English. The country's sufferings after Darien, and the general belief that all these had been caused by the London government's total lack of responsibility towards Scots except the few who were needed to keep the rest in suppression, gave Hamilton ample opportunity of developing his rhetoric and his popularity at Queensberry's expense.

Queensberry's tactic was to retreat slowly before the opposition's onslaughts, promising concessions and deferring the implementation of them, in the hope that, when no more was left to say, the indignation would abate to sullen passivity and some way might be found of buying Hamilton's support of the regime or manoeuvring him again into disrepute. A crucial vote went against him and he was forced to adjourn the House for three months. His opponents had talked themselves out, however, and when the session was resumed, with the help of the Earl of Argyll he succeeded in convincing a majority of the members that their interest would not be served by continued complaint of the king and his ministers, and a semblance of acceptance of things as they were was restored. Queensberry's parliamentary skills proved of more practical use than Hamilton's oratory and the relieved William rewarded him with the Knighthood of the Garter and promoted the helpful Earl of Argyll to duke.

Hamilton had lost the parliamentary contest but the people's discontents were strong as ever and he had not been silenced. When parliament met again Anne was queen and Queensberry once more Commissioner. It was to preserve the majority he had scratched together against Hamilton that Queensberry advised Anne to ignore the statutory requirement of an election after William's death, and we have seen how Hamilton protested against the illegality by leading a walk-out of his followers and a boycott of the rest of the session. An election could not be postponed indefinitely, however, even in those days, and in the election in the spring of 1703 votes for the opposition party – the Country Party of which Hamilton was now the acknowledged leader – were cast with as much emotion as if they had been stones hurled at Queensberry and the English.

When the new parliament met in Edinburgh in June 1703 the opposition had it all their own way. The government had done its best through its control of patronage to get the majority it needed but it found itself faced by a solid phalanx of nobles and commoners pledged under the banner of the Country Party to safeguard the Kirk and end or mend the union, and a cohort of Jacobites ready to play any game that would thwart the Hanover succession and keep the way open for young James Stuart at the Court of St Germains. The abortive discussions in London had shown there was no way of amending the union to the satisfaction of both countries; England, at full stretch in her efforts to keep Europe from falling under the domination of

Louis XIV, could not tolerate anything which threatened to end it. Queensberry's instructions from London were to hold the malcontents at bay as best he could. With no means of placating the Presbyterian critics of the union, he decided to try working with the Jacobites. The government was reconstructed to bring some of them in, their friends in exile were allowed to return, and plans were laid for putting Episcopalians on an equal footing in the community with Presbyterians. (Most Jacobites were Episcopalians or Catholics.) But the Edinburgh mob rioted, the Country Party stormed, the religious toleration proposal had to be dropped, and the alliance with the Jacobites was broken off. Country Party and Jacobites teamed up under the leadership of the Duke of Hamilton and the government was helplessly overwhelmed in the opposition flood.

Between July and September 1703 Hamilton and his supporters introduced and carried four measures calculated to set the English by the ears. First of all, to make their own position clear within Scotland itself and tell the English High Churchmen to cease interfering, the Country Party passed an act affirming the underlying loyalty of Scotland to the true Protestant religion and the Presbyterian way of running a Kirk. The Jacobites sat on their hands but the government could hardly oppose. Next they passed 'An Act anent Peace and War' forbidding the queen and the Privy Council to commit Scotland to war with any country without the consent of the Scottish parliament. This was aimed at England's war with France and the Jacobites supported it enthusiastically. It was followed by an act permitting any Scot who felt inclined to support England's enemies to do so by openly and legally importing French wines. English gentlemen whose appetites were stronger than their patriotism had to depend on smugglers for theirs. Lastly, they passed what they called an Act of Security, which provided that when Anne died the Scots parliament should appoint a successor who should be a Protestant and of royal lineage but *not* the same person as in England, unless the Scots had previously been satisfied that the process of government would be to their liking and had been guaranteed 'a free communication of trade, freedom of navigation, and the liberty of the plantations'. In the eyes of the Jacobites this put paid to the Hanoverian succession. They could not see the English conceding freedom of trade, and all that James Stuart would have to do to succeed to the throne of Scotland when the time came would be to change his religion.

While the four acts were being debated communications between London and Edinburgh became anxious, then feverish. Lord Godolphin, Anne's chief minister in London, to whom Queensberry was answerable, had been far too busy in the previous two years raising the money Marlborough needed for fighting the French to give much thought to the situation in Scotland. When he saw how things were developing in the summer of 1703 he became very alarmed. With the Scots in their present mood anything might happen. Anne's health was none too good: if she were to die the French were unlikely to miss the opportunity offered by this Act of Security to set up the Pretender in Scotland and menace England from another front besides the many on which she was already fighting – a front, moreover, on which she had no sea protection. If Marlborough's troops had to be brought back from Europe to fight the Scots aided by the French, England's continental allies would go down like ninepins and Louis' dominance of Western Europe and its colonial trade would be beyond challenge. The preservation of the union was vital to the safety of England. Godolphin's own parliamentary position was as weak as Queensberry's. To ask the Lords or the Commons to consider giving the Scots the freedom of English trade – their price for keeping the back door closed – was to court a resounding rebuff and lose all chance of persuading the Commons to go on providing the money for Marlborough's stand against Louis. All he could do was to pray fervently for Anne's survival and tell Queensberry to keep things going somehow until Marlborough could win a battle or two and show the Scots and the rest of the world that England was more than a match for France.

There was a way of playing for time. The Scots parliament might call its bills 'acts' and pass them against the wishes of the queen and her ministers, but none of them could get on the statute book until they had been touched by the queen's Commissioner in token of her royal assent. The only one of the acts passed by the rebels that really mattered was the Act of Security. The Act for Securing the True Protestant Religion was merely routine political tactics so far as Godolphin was concerned. The Act anent Peace and War was sterner stuff and irritated the English. But the only army Scotland could afford consisted of three thousand men who had to stay at home to keep the peace in that wild land. There was no other contribution she could make to England's war effort that was worth having except men who would go anywhere for a fight, and a lot of these were already among Marlborough's forces. It was insulting and annoying that Scotland should try to opt out of England's wars but the insult could be swallowed. The Wine Act was mere coat-trailing. More smuggled French wine was being drunk every month in England than Scotland could afford to buy in a year. There was no sense in needlessly inflaming the Scots parliamentarians and making heroes and martyrs out of nose-thumbers. Godolphin agreed that Queensberry should give the three acts the touch of the sceptre.

Queensberry was all for going on to approve the Act of Security. He was a queen's man, a union man and personally supported the Hanover succession. He was also a Scot and a politician. He had had no objection to playing a subservient role to London so long as he could be cock of the walk in Scotland. But he was acutely conscious of the mood of his countrymen and knew there was no future for him in Scots politics if he deserted them on the issue of making the union more profitable for Scotland. He argued that Godolphin should use the Scottish act to force the English parliament's hand. Godolphin would have none of it. His own future was at stake, as was that of his country. If anything had to be sacrificed, let it be Queensberry. Yet sacrifice might not be necessary for either of them, he suggested. It was September and the Scots parliament never sat in the winter. Let the act lie unsceptred on the table. Who knew what the position might be by another summer when the Scots politicians came out of their hibernation? The agitation might have died down. Marlborough might have won a victory. He himself might have a majority behind him in the English parliament. Queensberry knew that Anne would not agree to anything being done in her name which had not been approved by her English ministers. He bowed to the inevitable.

So in September 1703 the Scots parliament adjourned for the winter with its Act of Security unapproved, and Godolphin returned to his more important problem of saving the world from the French. The Duke of Hamilton and his Whig and Jacobite followers railed loudly against Anne, Godolphin, Queensberry and the whole machinery of a union which was all kicks and no ha'pence and which they had now been told they could not even arrange to terminate legally. They were not displeased, however, with the work of the most momentous and vociferous session the Edinburgh Parliament House had ever seen. A notice had been served on England beginning 'Dear Sirs, Unless – ' and they were determined it would never be withdrawn. They would be back next summer and God help the English if they continued to say them nay.

4 Blackmail before Blenheim

When the curtain went up next summer in the Parliament House in Edinburgh on Scene Two of the drama of the sundering union, the audience found that the leading Scottish actor had taken a startlingly different role. Sacked by London as unfit to go on playing chief champion of the union cause, the Duke of Queensberry seized a fiery cross and cast himself in a new part alongside the Duke of Hamilton as a leader of the rebels. Scotland had not napped peacefully while the parliamentary curtain was down, as Godolphin had hoped. On the contrary, there had been some very nasty manoeuvring behind the scenes, the repercussions of which had brought the English Lords and Commons almost to blows at Westminster and threatened to bounce Godolphin off his own stage.

An unprincipled Highland chief, Simon Fraser, Lord Lovat, was the mischief-maker. To buttress his claim to the family estates around the Moray Firth, in 1697, Fraser had abducted and tried to marry the real heiress, his nine years old third cousin. Thwarted in that scheme, he had seized, raped and married her mother, a sister of the Duke of Atholl. Outlawed in 1698 for these crimes, he had roamed about the Highlands until the Atholl family had forced him to flee in 1702 to France and the Jacobite Pretender's Court of St Germains. Taking advantage of the amnesty offered to Jacobite exiles in the previous year, he arrived in Edinburgh early in 1704 bent on making profit for himself somehow out of the current political situation. He carried in his pocket an unaddressed letter of recommendation from James II's widow. The idea had been that he should look around for some man of influence who could be won over to the Jacobite cause, or who could be of use to him in his work as a Jacobite agent, and present the letter as evidence of his standing at the court of the Pretender. Fraser cared little which side he worked for so long as he could

63

feather his own nest and foul someone else's. He decided both his objectives could be achieved by approaching Queensberry. Before doing so he wrote on the blank envelope of his letter the name of the Duke of Atholl.

The aim was diabolically clever. Atholl was Lord Privy Seal in the Duke of Queensberry's government but the family had behaved so equivocally in recent political history that it was not difficult to cast doubt on the reliability of his allegiance. The equivocations had begun with the duke's father, second Earl and first Marquess of Atholl, and chief of the clan Murray. In his younger days there had been no question of where he stood. In the Civil War he was a Royalist, led his clansmen in 1650 in an abortive attempt to rescue Charles II from the Covenanters, and fought against Cromwell until he was subdued by General Monck. After the Restoration the earl worked closely with Charles's Secretary for Scotland, the Duke of Lauderdale, and was the emissary through whom Lauderdale (as related in the previous chapter) had persuaded the Duke of Hamilton to drop his opposition to the royal tax demands by the promise – never honoured – that he would be given chief control of Scottish affairs. Atholl senior became successively a Privy Councillor, Lord Justice General, Captain of the Royal Guards, Lord Privy Seal, and a marquess. Falling out with Lauderdale over his harsh persecution of the conventicle preachers and congregations, he lost his post as Lord Justice General but was restored to it on Lauderdale's death. The Episcopalian Murrays had no love for the Presbyterian Campbells of Argyll. So, when the Earl of Argyll incurred Charles II's displeasure in 1684 and had to escape to Holland to avoid the executioner's axe, Atholl had himself appointed Lord Lieutenant of the Argyll territories in order to damage the Campbells as much as he could. He succeeded well. Hoping to lead a Presbyterian uprising against the newly enthroned James II, Argyll landed at Kintyre in his own lands but, when he failed to raise his clansmen as quickly as he had expected, Atholl took him prisoner and carried him off to Edinburgh where he was summarily beheaded. Campbell lands were thoroughly ravaged and the Privy Council had to intervene to stop Atholl from using his office of Lord Justice General to hang Argyll's second son, a sick man who had fallen into his hands. James II dubbed him a Knight of the Thistle for these services.

When William of Orange made his bid to supplant James, Atholl seems first to have been disposed to stand with James, then to have made an overture to William, and, when he found he was not too well received, to have gone some way back to James again. How the then Duke of Hamilton came out solidly for William, and the then Duke of Queensberry stuck by James, while their sons took opposite sides to the fathers, was described in the previous chapter. It was similar with the Atholl family. While the father was inclining towards James, his eldest son, Lord John Murray, hurried to offer himself to William. Atholl attended the convention of the estates which Hamilton had recommended and James's supporters nominated him to oppose Hamilton unsuccessfully for the chair. When his other efforts to frustrate the convention's purpose had come to naught and James had been dethroned, he joined the Duke of Queensberry in formally acquiescing in the offer of the crown to William and Mary. Then Viscount Dundee raised the standard for James and the moves made by the Murrays defied interpretation by either side. The marquess himself hurried from Scotland to Bath and sent a letter to the government telling them he had gone to the baths for his health, 'being troubled with violent pains'. He had left his castle at Blair Atholl, he said, in the care of his son – the Lord John Murray who had joined William. This did not deter Dundee from sending messengers to Lord John imploring him to hold the castle for James against the government forces advancing under General Mackay. He received no reply from Lord John but the marquess's right-hand man, a certain Stewart of Ballochin, hoisted the Jacobite colours over the castle. Lord John surrounded it with about fifteen hundred clansmen. The clan were ready to fight to oust Ballochin but, when they discovered they were expected to haul down King James's flag and substitute King William's, they retreated to a river in which they drank King James's health and went home. The advancing General Mackay sent a message to Lord John that, if King William's flag was not flying over Blair Castle when his men reached it, they would take it by force and hang Stewart of Ballochin from any wall that might be left standing. If Lord John helped Ballochin in any way, anything left of the castle and its contents would be burned to the ground. Thus sternly adjured, Lord John tried again to change the flags but, as only a couple of hundred of his clan could be assembled to assist him, the attempt was abandoned and most of the Murrays marched off under the marquess's third son, Lord James, and were with Dundee at Killiecrankie when the Highlanders overwhelmed Mackay's soldiers but lost their leader and all hope of recovering the throne for James. The marquess protested from the waters at Bath that his clan had betrayed him by taking the losing side. As he produced no evidence that he had ever ordered them not to do so, nobody believed him. Macaulay went so far as to call him 'the falsest, the most fickle, the most pusillanimous of mankind', a somewhat harsh denunciation of a Highland chief who was only anxious to be on the winning side.

General Mackay was not alone in doubting which side Lord John had been on in the comedy at Blair Castle. He was strongly suspected by many of trying to play the same equivocal game as his father. He seems to have been able to convince some influential members of the government of his sincerity, however, for in 1693 he was given an appointment to inquire into the circumstances of the Glencoe massacre, and in the following year he became joint Secretary of State for Scotland alongside the Earl of Seafield. Two years later William created him Earl of Tullibardine and Lord High Commissioner. His father must have thought the policy of playing both ends of the table was paying off. The new Earl of Tullibardine was politically astute, but he suffered from an un-governable temper when thwarted in anything he had set his heart on, and he suddenly resigned after holding the Commissionership for two years when his nominee was not appointed Lord President of the Court of Session. He was out of office for the remaining four years of William's reign and saw himself overtaken by Queensberry.

Queensberry wanted his support in the 1703 Parliament and brought him into the ministry in the spring of that year as Lord Privy Seal. A month afterwards, when his father died, Queen Anne took the opportunity of binding him closer to her admini-strations by raising his marquessate to a dukedom. But the equivocating tendency of the Murrays re-asserted itself. To Queensberry's disgust, the speeches of the Lord Privy Seal in the debates on the Act of Security began to echo many of the senti-ments of the Duke of Hamilton. He was not wholly surprised. When there were two camps in the country, it was to be expected that the head of the house of Atholl should be trying to be in both

of them. He was considering how to rid himself of this dubious
ally when Simon Fraser wrote the duke's name on his letter and
offered it as evidence that Atholl was in secret league with the
Courts of St Germains and Versailles and betraying the government of which he was a member. Fraser could back his accusations
with intimate personal knowledge of the correspondence which
was passing between the Jacobite Pretender and those members
of the Scottish and English nobility who thought it safer, in case
the Pretender might one day make the throne again, to have
shown themselves to be not unfriendly. One of these was the Duke
of Hamilton, who had led the fight for the Act of Security; if
Fraser could get Queensberry to believe that Atholl was secretly
allied with Hamilton to use the Act of Security for the Pretender's
cause, Queensberry would probably not hesitate about using the
information to bring both these formidable political rivals down.
In which case, he would be grateful to Fraser, whose political
fortune would be made while Anne lived and also in the event
of a Hanover succession. If Anne died and if the Pretender's star
should then shine, Fraser could maintain that he had been acting
throughout as a faithful Jacobite agent who had endeavoured to
insinuate himself into Queensberry's good graces to serve his
master's cause by sabotaging Scottish politics. Should the plot
misfire in any way, all would not be lost if Atholl were tumbled
down.

The scheme went well to begin with. Queensberry accepted
the letter at face value, took Fraser into his pay, and sent him off
to the Highlands to play the Jacobite agent and collect evidence
against more of Queensberry's political rivals and opponents. The
duke then took the letter to Queen Anne and Godolphin and
denounced Atholl and Hamilton as conspiring Jacobites. At this
point Fraser blundered. There was a man in Scotland named
Robert Ferguson, known as 'The Plotter', who had been mixed
up in every conspiracy in England and Scotland in the preceding
thirty years. Elated with his success, Fraser boasted of it to
Ferguson. Ferguson's professional jealousy was roused: he
hurried to tell Atholl and Hamilton, who started shouting their
innocence from the house-tops. Immediately Scotland was in an
uproar. Queensberry was violently attacked on all sides for conspiring with a known rascal like Fraser to destroy his political
rivals. Atholl appealed to the queen, protesting his innocence and

loyalty. A Privy Council meeting was held in London at which Queensberry and Atholl confronted one another. To his surprise Atholl found his protestations of innocence of any treasonable correspondence were not being wholly believed by his colleagues, and in a rage he resigned.

The Scots had put themselves under a general suspicion of disloyalty in English eyes by their refusal to commit themselves to the Hanover succession. Here now was evidence that at least one member of the Scottish government was actively conspiring with the enemy. Demands were made in London that he should be tried and punished. The House of Lords, with a Whig majority, took up the cry to embarrass Tory Godolphin.

Godolphin tried hard to damp the clamour down. To charge and try the Duke of Atholl in Edinburgh was to invite a popular uprising by all the Scottish malcontents; to attempt to take any action against him in London was to challenge the nominal independence of Scotland and the whole basis of the existing union, and possibly to drive the Scots into total repudiation of it. The Whig peers were aware of the impasse into which they were forcing Godolphin but the chance to roast the Tories in the fire of mob fury was too good to be passed over. They ignored the constitutional difficulties and pointed to the close friendship between Atholl and the Earl of Nottingham, a Secretary of State in the Godolphin ministry. It was also known that Atholl was keen to marry his son to one of Marlborough's daughters and that the good offices of Godolphin, whose son had married another of the Marlborough girls, had been sought to aid the match. As Marlborough was also a Tory, from the angle of party politics there seemed to be ample ground for believing in a concerted Tory effort to clear Atholl's name. The peers resolved by a majority to set up an inquiry into the whole affair. However, there was a Tory majority in the Commons: correspondence with the Court of St Germains was not a sin in Tory eyes and there was no telling what embarrassments for the party a Whig-controlled inquiry might dredge up. The Commons therefore protested to the queen that the Lords inquiry was an insult to the throne and an invasion of the royal prerogative. There was no doubt as to which side Queen Anne leant, as a Tory, in the constitutional wrangle. The Lords reply was to publish the case for an inquiry for the whole country to see and in the course of their revelations they accused the entire Scottish nation of encouraging Jacobite plotting against the throne by their refusal to endorse the Hanovarian succession. The Scots were enraged. The English House of Lords was daring to comment on Scottish affairs and tell an independent nation what it ought to do to give England peace of mind. It was now obvious that the storm was about to blow too dangerously hard to bring any party advantage in a country at war, and Atholl's resignation was allowed to end it.

It gave a vigorous toss, however, to the line-up in Scottish politics. There was no reason to suppose that Atholl had really been guilty of anything more treasonable in his flirtations with the Pretender than dozens of other politicians of his time, including Godolphin and Marlborough themselves. They were all insuring against any awkward turn of events. But the Scots duke had a haughty, passionate temper, and in his rage against Queensberry and resentment of the Whig attack, he threw over all his previous political connections and announced himself as henceforth the out-and-out Jacobite they had said he was, a supporter of the Act of Security, an opponent of the Hanovarian succession, and an enemy of union, however amended, under any but a Stuart monarch.

At the same time the Duke of Queensberry lost his job. Anne and Godolphin could not forgive him for involving them in the mess over Atholl, and his ministry in Scotland had broken up. So they dismissed him, and put in his place the Marquess of Tweeddale, who had been one of the leaders in the previous summer of the movement to end or mend the union. His father had played an unhappy part in the political events of the previous decade. Never very comfortable under Charles II and James because of his sympathies with the Covenanters, he had gone over quickly to William of Orange, and as Chancellor had given the royal assent to the Glencoe Massacre in 1692 while William had been away on the continent. Consequently he had been reviled by the people and in an effort to regain esteem while acting as Lord High Commissioner in 1695 he had strongly supported the Darien venture. When William found it necessary to disavow that scheme to avoid falling out with Spain, Tweeddale senior was made the scapegoat, dismissed from office, and died a year later. The son had joined the Duke of Hamilton in the Country Party. He was not an able politician, being too simple and straightforward for the party intrigues of the day, but he was generally liked as well-intentioned and honest, even by opponents. Lockhart of Carnwath thought him 'the least ill-meaning man of his party either through inclination or capacity'. He was a solid Presbyterian, however, and favoured union under the Hanoverian succession if it could be arranged on terms more acceptable to Scotland. During the winter, with some twenty other members of parliament, he had come to the conclusion that endorsement by Scotland of the Hanover succession was an essential precondition of any successful negotiation with the English about amending the union. They had formed a new party which the wits of the Scottish capital were dubbing the 'Squadrone Volante', the flying squadron, a pun on their airy detachment from the other parties and their supposed willingness to go anywhere or do anything which served their own interest. Tweeddale and the Squadrone offered to Godolphin that if they were given the responsibilities of government in Edinburgh they would undertake to have the Hanover succession on the Scottish statute book before the end of the coming summer session. Godolphin advised Anne to make the leaders of the group her Scottish ministers.

So when the actors took their places on the stage for the Scottish parliament's 1704 summer season, the Marquess of Tweeddale had taken over as leading man, the Dukes of Hamilton and Atholl were jostling one another for leadership of the opposition, and the dismissed Duke of Queensberry was believed to be sulking somewhere around the theatre. Simon Fraser, whose villainies had played such havoc with the original casting, had scuttled back to France where, despite his justifiable claims to have properly bedevilled English and Scottish politics as a good Jacobite agent should, he was thrown into gaol. If the London management of Anne and Godolphin had thought the Duke of Queensberry would let the play go on in Edinburgh without him, they were sadly mistaken. Hissing from the wings into the ears of Atholl and Hamilton, he suggested that if they would agree to forget how badly he had behaved in the Fraser affair, he would join them in routing Tweeddale and the Squadrone Volante and their proposed passage into law of the Hanover succession. Atholl and Hamilton knew Queensberry was the ablest parliamentarian of the lot of them. Agreement was quickly reached and when the curtain rose Queensberry, to the consternation of Tweeddale, leapt from the shadows into the limelight and began loudly improvising a new part of the patriot saviour of his country, much to the delight of the Scottish groundlings. The noise made by the ducal trio drowned the pleas of the Squadrone Volante for acceptance of the House of Hanover. In very quick time the Edinburgh Parliament had again passed by an overwhelming majority the Act of Security announcing the determination of the Scots to have a ruler of their own – unless the English gave them an Open Sesame to the wealth from which they had been so meanly and brutally barred.

So Queen Anne had again to face the grave dilemma: should she give the act the touch of her sceptre as queen of Scotland and sign what would seem to be the death-warrant of the union of the crowns, risking popular outcry and political upheaval in her England at war with France, or should she listen to her entirely English heart, again refuse the touch, and burst the union asunder with an insurrection in Scotland which would almost certainly bring her brother and his French allies into the country and lay England open to invasion through the back-door? While she debated the question anxiously with Godolphin the Edinburgh parliament twisted the screw. They informed her that so long as she withheld her approval of the act they would withhold supplies for her expenses in Scotland. No touch, no cash.

Nothing at all had come to Godolphin's rescue in the year's breathing-space he had ordered Queensberry to make for him. His parliamentary position was in little better shape than the luckless Tweeddale's. There was still a Whig majority in the Lords which would never agree to anything that might weaken England in the fight with the French, and the Commons majority of his own party was split in factions and certainly would not follow him in anything that could placate the Scots. The war with France was at a desperately critical stage. To save Vienna Marlborough had marched his army from the Netherlands through Germany and arrested the French advance in Bavaria. Another French army under the great Marshal Tallard was hastening to crush him. His ally Prince Eugene of Savoy was committed to holding back still another French army on the Rhine. There was dissension with other allied commands. In Italy the Duke of Savoy's position

seemed hopeless and a force of Hungarian rebels was menacing
Vienna from the other side. The fate of all Europe hung on
Marlborough. If the French reached Vienna the alliance of
Dutch, Austrians, Germans, Savoyards, and other miscellaneous
small states that Marlborough and Godolphin had held together
for four difficult years would collapse. Louis would be undisputed
master of Europe and the English army would either have to
surrender in the Black Forest or be utterly destroyed trying to
fight an impossible way back to the coast. Marlborough had
beaten one mixed French and Bavarian army at the Schellenberg
but no one could expect him to hold back three. If his army were
wiped out, Godolphin's government would fall, since he had
backed Marlborough's gamble against the opposition of most of
his party. What would then happen to England?

It was against this background of impending doom that in the
first week of August 1704 Godolphin had to advise Anne what to
do about the Scots. The matter of financial supply was petty but
crucial, as the Duke of Queensberry knew. The Scottish Treasury
was empty. If no money was voted, the Scottish army of three
thousand men could not be paid and would disband. Without
them to keep law and order the rabble-rousers would have it all
their own way. Rebellion and anarchy would be let loose. Lord
Seafield, the most circumspect member of the Scottish government, had sent Godolphin a serious warning. If the Act of
Security were not immediately approved and the funds released,
the government would be powerless to prevent an insurrection
and the French invasion that would follow. The amount of money
required was a bagatelle for Godolphin, accustomed to finding
the huge sums Marlborough had been spending, and he offered
to advance it to Tweeddale's government. They advised against.
The dukes had made it clear that acceptance of a loan from
England would be regarded as an evasion of the will of the
Scottish parliament, would be unconstitutional and the signal for
open revolt.

The situation was a maddening one for the Englishman. The
Scots were blackmailing him, under threat of opening their doors
to the enemy, into advising the queen to approve an act which
would give them full statutory authority to blackmail him or his
successors in the same way unless they were bought off in the mean-
time with the right, as his fellow-countrymen saw it, of picking

England's pockets. At a moment when England was facing disaster and humiliation Scotland was putting the squeeze on him by means of a paltry sum that might be exchanged any night at London's gaming tables. It was a monstrous piece of blackguardism. If only Marlborough could perform a miracle and come up with a resounding victory! The news from Bavaria was bad, however. Two of the French armies had joined and Marlborough's doom seemed sealed. With so evil a day just ahead wisdom counselled postponing another. Godolphin shrugged his shoulders, swallowed his spleen, and advised the queen to approve. The royal consent was given on August 5.

Three days earlier, unknown to anybody in London, Marlborough had performed the wanted miracle. He had come up with a tremendous victory. Aided by a swift and totally unexpected movement which he had arranged with Prince Eugene, he had smashed the might of Louis at Blenheim, saved Vienna and the alliance, and averted all immediate danger to England. The news was brought to London as fast as horses could gallop. It arrived too late to cheat the three Scottish dukes of their satisfaction. Anne, Godolphin and all England were too relieved and jubilant to care for the moment how gallingly fate had conspired with the blackmailers.

The Scots were also celebrating their victory. The English might have every reason to be pleased with themselves but Louis was not dead yet and one battle, however glorious, might not win the war. Anne's approval of the Act of Security had returned to them the key of England's back-door.

5 The Brink of War

By January 1705 the tensions between the Scots and the English had mounted so high that the two countries were teetering on the brink of war.

The High Tories in England set the ball rolling. They hated Godolphin. They hated him because the queen and the moderates of the party accepted him as a Tory, and everything he did stamped him in their eyes as a Whig. They hated him because he had made it politically possible for England to send a professional army (something she should never have) over to the continent (where no English soldiers should ever go) to fight against France (with which England should be friends) for reasons no Englishman could support (unless he were a Whig). They hated him for making it financially possible (at their expense) for Marlborough to hold his grand alliance together (to nobody's grandeur but his own). They hated him because Marlborough's victory had raised him and his Whig and moderate Tory followers high in popular favour and confounded their arguments against the war. They had been casting around for three years for a chance to unseat him. His advice to Anne to approve the Scottish Act of Security gave them their opportunity. When the national excitement over Blenheim began to die down they launched the attack.

Godolphin was very vulnerable. He had given way to the Scots to save England from attack from behind, in what he believed to be a moment of great national peril. The High Tories brushed aside such a notion. What peril could England have been in when Blenheim had already been won? It was little use Godolphin's protesting that he did not know Blenheim had been won. He ought to have known what Marlborough and England were capable of, retorted his assailants. In any case, why give in to blackmail from – of all people – those miserable paupers, the Scots? The glory of Blenheim had been sullied by a snivelling

surrender to the empty threats of breechless beggars. Godolphin
had shown rank, indefensible cowardice and England had been
gratuitously humiliated. He deserved to be impeached and shot
or hanged as a traitor to his country. The rhetoric came oddly
from politicians who had been against Marlborough's fighting any
battles at all in Europe, and who opposed the Hanoverian succession which the Scottish act was avoiding. The High Tories were
blind to any incongruities in the attitudes they were striking. They
were in full cry after two of their bitter hates – Godolphin and
the Presbyterian Scots. They were also heedless of the consequences
to England if they brought Godolphin down. Marlborough had
insisted before accepting the allied command against the French
that Godolphin, the only man he trusted, should be in command
at home. It was possible that if Godolphin fell Marlborough
would throw in his hand. The war against Louis was very far from
being won and without Marlborough and Godolphin England's
chances of controlling the Grand Monarch's ambitions seemed
slim. To hell with Europe and the war, the High Tories seemed
to be saying to one another, down with Godolphin and the Scots.

The High Tory leaders were Anne's uncle, the Earl of
Rochester, who had been dismissed by his niece from the Lord
Lieutenancy of Ireland because of his hostility to Marlborough
and opposition to the war, and the Earl of Nottingham, who had
resigned a few months earlier from Godolphin's ministry over the
policy that had led to Blenheim. A dark and melancholy man, he
had never concealed his dislike of Marlborough and the Lord
Treasurer. Godolphin's only ally among the able and influential
members of the party was Robert Harley, who was allowed by
the practice of the time to combine the Speakership of the
Commons with being Godolphin's right-hand man in the ministry.
While Godolphin managed the large affairs of state Harley pulled
the strings that had so far held the moderates of the party
sufficiently together. He was a man of mystery and intrigue, a
button-holer in the lobbies and on the backstairs, employer of
secret intelligence agents and propagandists (among them Daniel
Defoe, journalist and creator of Robinson Crusoe). On this
occasion Rochester and Nottingham had him well beaten.
Thanks to Blenheim, there was no immediate military danger to
help rally the moderate Tories who had supported Godolphin as
a war leader in the two previous years, and they were free at last

to join their more rabid brethren and give full vent to pent-up animosities against Scots, nonconformists, war-profiteers, the Duchess of Marlborough, and anything else that maintaining Godolphin in power had required them to tolerate. The cries of treason and impeachment had raised the party blood-pressure and Harley had nothing to whisper in anybody's ear that would bring it down. Godolphin seemed doomed, since the Whigs could hardly be expected to come to his rescue. Queen Anne was prostrated with anxiety. Where was she to find another acceptable chief minister? She could not possibly take a Whig and it would be insufferable to have to reward Rochester and Nottingham for hounding out Godolphin. What was to happen to her Marlborough, her England? She cursed the Scots for their intransigence and their wretched Act of Security.

The peak of the Tory denunciation of their leader was reached at the end of November in a full-dress debate in the Lords, which Anne attended in the vain hope that her presence would have a restraining effect on Godolphin's accusers. It was opened by Lord Haversham, no mincer of his words, and he did everything to Godolphin his hearers had expected of him. When Godolphin rose to reply it was obvious that he was badly shaken and far below his usual form. He spoke haltingly, attempting no real defence of himself, pleading only that he had been trying to avert a revolt of the Scots. Overflowing with the confidence of hindsight, peer after peer on the Tory side belaboured and bludgeoned him for being so timid and hasty, so devoid of the courage of an Englishman and the prudence of a statesman, when a delay of a day would have been enough to let him thumb his nose at the Scots and their Act of Security. England had been shamed. Scotland must now be humiliated and brought to heel. Nobody found a good word for Godolphin. The real gravity of his crime in all their eyes was that it was the contemptible Scots to whom he had given in and from the way Godolphin hung his head it appeared he was prepared to lie down under this ignominious charge.

The Whigs seemed in two minds. Lord Somers, ex-Lord Chancellor, had nothing to say in Godolphin's excuse but counselled moderation of the abuse of the Scots. England had no legal jurisdiction over Scotland. The wild talk of humiliation and punishment could only inflame the relations between the peoples. Let the Scots keep their act, he advised, but find a way of hitting them where it would hurt most – in their nearly empty pockets. The Earl of Halifax, whose money had won him a place in the Whig aristocracy, curtly dismissed the cautious lawyer's advice and plunged into a virulent execration of Scotland and Godolphin. The High Tories chuckled and beamed. If his was to be the voice of the Whigs, nothing could save Godolphin or such peace as remained between the Scots and the English. While Halifax was still on his feet, Lord Wharton, another Whig, slid over to the government bench and began to whisper earnestly with Godolphin.

Halifax was respected as a financial genius but he was not popular in his party. Wharton was, except with the husbands of young and attractive wives. Descendant of a Puritan family to whom he owed his Whig politics and loathing of the High Tories, he had in his private life abandoned everything else of his heritage for the manners, morals and fashions of a Restoration libertine. Now in his fifties, he had behind him a record of debauchery and deceit which entitled his political enemies to regard him as the most villainous blackguard of his day. He had kept his looks, his humour and his charm, however, and he had two other qualities which greatly commended him to political friends. He was a brilliant organiser of elections and party warfare and he was the soul of honour in public affairs to all on his side. The Tories therefore had reason for apprehension when they saw him in close conclave with Godolphin. It was evident from the sudden lifting of Godolphin's beaten expression that Wharton must be putting forward an interesting proposition. Godolphin had fought the French war with far more support from the Whigs than from his own party. On that issue he had really been one of them. It would be in keeping with Wharton's conflicting reputations as a cad and a gentleman if he were now offering the battered chief minister a means of staying on his feet. The Whigs had a majority in the Lords. If Godolphin found their way out acceptable he could be saved.

To the intense chagrin of all his enemies, saved he was. The scheme which the alliance of Wharton and Somers, Godolphin and Harley proceeded to argue through the English parliament in a series of debates over the next three months turned the Scots' threat back on themselves. The Scottish Act of Security had demanded equality of trade, or the union would be broken when Anne should die. The retaliatory act which the English parliament passed in March 1705 was entitled 'An Act for the effectual securing the Kingdom of England from the apparent dangers which may arise from several Acts lately passed by the Parliament of Scotland' and told the Scots that if they had not accepted the House of Hanover before Christmas the union would be suspended there and then, to the extent that all Scots setting foot in England would be treated as aliens unless they became naturalised Englishmen or joined the armed forces; no Scottish cattle, horses, linen or coal would be allowed into England; no English wool would be exported to Scotland; and the navy would stop all trade between Scotland and France. If the Scots accepted the Hanoverian succession by the stated dead-line, commissioners would be appointed by the Queen to negotiate new union arrangements.

The scheme was ingenious. It put the Scots effectively on the spot. Either they had to accept Hanover by Christmas or face a deeper impoverishment, for the banned animals and goods made up the bulk of their exports and without English wool they would lose some profitable manufacture. Even the most bloodthirsty Scot-haters among the High Tories had to agree that there was something to be said for these sanctions. The scheme was enough to save Godolphin's face and power because it separated again the pro-war moderate Tories from the anti-war Tories. It averted any danger of Marlborough's resignation and the collapse of the alliance. Anne was immensely relieved at the reprieve of Godolphin, but her debt to the Whigs left a sour taste in her mouth.

While the Alien Act, as it was dubbed for short, was being debated in England tempers in Scotland rose perilously high. Scots who knew what was in prospect for them were against waiting for the English parliament to decide to starve them into submission. 'Invade England Now' became the cry. The Act of Security had provided for arming a national militia. Throughout the lowlands in the early months of 1705 bands of angry men met twice a week at every parish church door for military training. In Ayrshire, twenty years earlier the county of the most militant Covenanters, seven thousand men were reported to be fully armed and drilling for a southward march. In the Highlands, chiefs were warning their clansmen to be ready. Presbyterians were consorting with Jacobite Catholics and Episcopalians and agreeing to forget their religious antipathies in a common determination to have out with the English whatever grievance they had against life on the less fortunate side of the border. Reports and rumours of these activities started a panic in the English northern counties, which saw themselves defenceless against the Scots. Demands were sent to Parliament for arms. The Lords voted for repairs to the fortifications at Newcastle, Carlisle and Hull and for arming a militia force in Northumberland, Cumberland, Westmoreland, Durham, Yorkshire and Lancashire, but the Commons rejected the militia plan as being too dangerous in an area where there were many Catholic and pro-Jacobite landowners who might be tempted to join the Scots in rejecting the House of Hanover. They preferred to consider the possibility of bringing back Marlborough's army in the event of an attack. Southern England remained relatively unmoved: the Scots were a long way off, its inhabitants had fewer folk memories of invaders from the north, and they regarded Scotsmen with a rancorous contempt. At the same time as the Commons passed the clauses in the Alien Act which would ban Scottish linen from England and Ireland, they deliberately and gratuitously inflamed the Scots even farther by opening the West Indian colonies to Irish linen. Had such a concession been granted to the Scots, there might never have been an Act of Security.

A few weeks after the passage of the Alien Act the Scots disgraced themselves by committing a shocking outrage against humanity. To save their own skins from the Edinburgh rabble, the Scottish Privy Council rejected the claims of justice and the commands of Queen Anne and hanged three Englishmen on Leith sands for a crime of which the Council had proof they were innocent. 'A more fearful example of mob law never occurred in a civilised country,' say Dicey and Rait, two of the most cold-blooded of Scots historians. It is probable, however, that if the Council had not given way to the demands of the mob, the mad march of the Edinburghers would not have stopped round a lynch-gallows on the Forth sands but would have carried down across the border taking with it the thousands who were drilling and arming. War between the Scots and the English would have begun.

The passionate fury that raged through Scotland over the Englishmen had earlier origins than the Alien Act. It had all begun a year before when a Scottish ship, the *Annandale*, was seized in the Downs by the English navy and impounded, on the ground that its owners had breached the privileges of the East India Company by enlisting English sailors for a voyage to India on behalf of the now almost moribund Scottish Africa Company, which had engaged in the luckless Darien adventure. Its Welsh skipper had peached to the East India managers and they had appealed to the Godolphin government. The news of the seizure set up a commotion in Scotland, where the Africa Company shareholders saw it as yet another evidence of England's determination to bar them from the wealth of the Orient. All the efforts of the Scottish government to persuade their London masters to make restitution were vain.

While the Scots were cursing their impotence something happened which was taken by the godly to mean that Providence was giving them a chance to get their own back. An English ship, the *Worcester*, put into Leith. It was on its way home to London heavily laden with a rich cargo from Calcutta and its skipper, Captain Green, had gone round the north of Scotland to avoid the French privateers in the Channel. He intended to wait in Leith until he could sail in convoy with other vessels southward bound. The Scots leaped to the conclusion that the *Worcester* must be an East India Company ship, and Roderick Mackenzie, the secretary of the Africa Company, hired a gang of men to make friendly overtures to the crew, worm their way on board, capture the ship and take it across the Firth of Forth to Burntisland in Fife. The plan succeeded but the *Worcester* turned out to be a privately owned ship, trading as illegally with India as the *Annandale*, and neither the East India Company nor the English government was moved in any way by its seizure. The Scots were reluctant to release their prize but were unable to decide what to do with it. For several months it lay under guard at Burntisland while the crew passed the time drinking in the pubs of Edinburgh and Leith, and regaling the impoverished Scots frequenters with tales of their adventures in pursuit of the wealth of the Indies. During this time another Scottish ship, the *Speedy Return*, which had also been on a sneak voyage to India, became overdue and rumours began to spread that the *Worcester* was responsible. Hints had been dropped by some of the crew, the story ran, that Captain Green had turned pirate on his voyage home, intercepted the *Speedy Return*, sunk it, and murdered Captain Drummond and all his men. The frustrated Africa Company secretary saw an opportunity of sequesting the *Worcester*'s valuable cargo and worked on public prejudice until the Scottish Privy Council were forced to order the *Worcester*'s crew to be arrested and tried.

The trial took place in the early months of 1705 when the Alien Act was in its final stages in the English parliament, and a fever of hostility to the English was coursing through every Scotsman's veins. Scarcely anybody inside the court or out of it cared a button for justice for the Englishmen. The whole country was clamouring for revenge for everything the English had ever done to them and it was the entire hated English nation they saw standing in the dock in Edinburgh. There was no evidence to support the charges, except a missing ship about whose whereabouts or fate nothing was known, and statements alleged to have been made by the ship's doctor and a coloured member of the crew that they believed Captain Drummond to have been done to death by Captain Green and others. It was all heresay. No witness was produced who had seen the murder or Drummond or the missing ship. The doctor and the other witness obviously had grievances against Green and contradicted one another in their evidence. The Privy Council sent six peers on a mission to Burntisland to examine the *Worcester*'s cargo and bring back evidence to support the piracy charge. They returned empty-handed. Nevertheless, on March 21, a week after the Alien Act went on the English statute book, a verdict of guilty was returned against Green and fourteen of the crew, and they were condemned to be hanged in batches on Leith sands over a period of three weeks to give the crowds of crazed Scots plenty of time to soak their gall in spectacles of English suffering. 'All people', wrote Defoe, recording the Scottish reaction, 'seemed to acknowledge a wonderful and invisible hand in it, directing and pointing out the detecting some horrible crime, which vengeance suffered not to go unpunished.'

The trial had created a fuss in England, of course, and in consequence evidence came forward to refute utterly the piracy and murder charges. Sailors from the *Speedy Return* were alive and well in England and told their story. The *Speedy Return* had indeed been attacked in the Indian Ocean by pirates but they had come from Madagascar and the attack had taken place at a time when the *Worcester* was known to have been far from the scene. Captain Drummond had not been murdered but had been carried off to Madagascar where, as far as could be ascertained, he was still held. This information was actually secured and made known to members of the Squadrone government before the verdicts were returned, but popular frenzy was at too high a pitch for them to be willing to intervene.

Reluctant as the Godolphin-Wharton combination were to add any more combustible material to the fire they had lit with the Alien Act, they could not ignore the human sacrifice the Scots seemed determined to make of fifteen demonstrably innocent Englishmen. Anne had just appointed the young Scots Whig, John Campbell, Duke of Argyll, to be her Commissioner in Scotland. Bold, forthright and soldierly, he was not the man to truckle to mob-rule. He was convinced of the innocence of the *Worcester* men and persuaded Anne and Godolphin to allow him to write from London to the Earl of Seafield, the Scottish Lord Chancellor, instructing him to delay the executions until a formal inquiry could be made into the evidence, which suggested a miscarriage of justice. Anne followed up with a letter of her own to Seafield telling him that she was studying a report on the *Worcester* affair, and she assumed no action would be taken until she had had time to make her wishes known.

Seafield had the reputation among his political enemies of falling over himself to keep on the right side of royalty. The second son of the third Earl of Findlater, he had been called to the bar in 1685 and had supported King James, but had been brought into William's government by the third Duke of Hamilton and made Solicitor General in 1693. Since then he had never been out of office, however ministries had changed, because no government felt able to do without his talents as a lawyer and politician, and because these were so readily at the disposal of the government of the day. Lockhart says he was 'so entirely abandoned to serve the court measures, be they what they will, that he seldom or never consulted his own inclinations, but was a blank sheet of paper which the court might fill up with what they pleased.' Always willing to be fair, however, the same writer describes him as 'finely accomplished, a learned lawyer, a just judge, courteous and good-natured.' Macky saw him 'very beautiful in his person, with a graceful behaviour, smiling countenance, and a soft tongue. He affects plainness and familiarity in his conversation, but is not sincere.' He had opposed the Darien scheme after it fell foul of King William and the mob had in consequence broken his windows while the Duke of Argyll's father denounced him as having 'neither honour, honesty, friendship, nor courage.' The duke's contempt hurt him no more than the mob's stones. He was created Viscount Seafield in 1698 and Earl in 1701, Lord High Chancellor in 1702.

Seafield was, as Lockhart affirms, a learned lawyer and a just judge. He had no illusions about the *Worcester* business. He knew the trial had been a farce. His judgment as a lawyer, as well as his inclination as a successful courtier and politician, told him he should heed the queen and Argyll. But he knew the mood of his countrymen, particularly in Edinburgh, and that they had not forgiven his opposition to Darien. He felt he should not be asked to shoulder the sole responsibility, at the dangerous Scottish end, for an order they would regard as robbing them of just vengeance for their national wrongs. He called a meeting of the Privy Council for the day before the first executions. Neither the Marquess of Tweeddale nor any other of the Squadrone Volante ministers still in office turned up. They were all indisposed or otherwise detained. There were, however, fifteen other Councillors present and Seafield read them the queen's letter and the affidavits of the *Speedy Return* sailors which had accompanied it. He put the question to the vote: to hang or not to hang. Three voted for a reprieve, three against, nine refused to vote one way or the other. Seafield was in a serious dilemma since he held a casting vote. The reason for the absences and the abstentions was abundantly clear. It had been difficult to make a way to the council chamber because of the press of the crowd in the street, shouting the fearful things they would do if the Council dared to baulk them of the orgy they had been promised by the court of law. His ministerial colleagues were safe enough on their country estates. The mob were unlikely to worry about who had voted for or against or had the caution to abstain. Nor would they overlook the significance of the coincidence that there were fifteen present in the room. If he cast his vote for reprieve he might be presenting the crowd outside with fifteen substitutes for the fifteen lives he was voting to save. Nor would these lives be saved. If he decided to see justice done the result could be that thirty men would unjustly die. The silence must have been tense as they waited for him to make up his mind. He found a compromise between his conscience as a lawyer and his responsibility for their safety. He said he would sign the reprieve if a majority were prepared to sign with him. Each Privy Councillor studied the others and weighed up the chances. Six, perhaps brave, perhaps taking a calculated risk, intimated they were willing. Eight shook their heads.

Seafield still hesitated. It was against all his instincts to surrender to a mob. There were larger and more urgent matters at stake, however, than the delicacies of his make-up or even his concern for justice or his reputation in the eyes of posterity or at the judgement seat. It was he who had warned Godolphin in the previous year that there would be bloody insurrection in Scotland if the Act of Security were stopped from becoming law. For every man who would have been ready to strike then there were now twenty, perhaps a hundred. War with England would be total madness for the Scots since it could bring them nothing but defeat and humiliation without French intervention, and who could say how that might end for the whole island. He leaned to closer union as the solution of the countries' conflicts and in spite of the Act of Security and the Alien Act was eager to work for it. If the border were crossed before reasonable men like himself on both sides of it could get together, all hope of reconciliation would be over for his lifetime, perhaps indefinitely, and the way he ended this meeting could precipitate the crisis. He suggested they put off the final decision until the morrow and meet just before the hour set for the first batch of executions. The mob relaxed when they heard no reprieves had been granted and the Privy Councillors were allowed to go their ways with no more than some rough exhortations to stay of that mind.

The following morning it seemed that everybody from the country round had come into Edinburgh to see the first men die. It was estimated that there were at least eighty thousand in the streets carrying guns, swords and sticks. When the Privy

Council reassembled in Holyrood the number present had fallen to eleven. Seafield compared the numbers inside and outside and shrugged his shoulders. The issue was obviously beyond his control. Why be squeamish about judicial murder? They were peers and gentlemen. The victims of their injustice were mere seamen whose lives were necessarily cheap. His duty was to keep the peace for as long as he could. If that meant slaughtering the innocents, it was unfortunate; better that than being slaughtered himself. It was announced to the crowd that the day's victims would be Captain Green, John Mather and James Simpson.

Unhappily for Seafield, it had got abroad that he had hesitated to authorise the death sentences. This information travelled through the crowd around the Tolbooth and in the High Street and became magnified into a report that Seafield had persuaded the Council to grant reprieves. Seafield's coach had left Holyrood while the names of the men to be hanged were being announced and, the crowd being thinner in the Canongate, it reached the Tron Kirk before the news had been passed along to the denser mob there. Recognising the Lord Chancellor, infuriated men stormed round him smashing the windows and overturning the vehicle. His desperate shouts that the Englishmen were to die were ignored and he was pulled from the coach. He would have been struck down and torn to pieces if some of his friends had not managed to thrust him into a house from which they succeeded in assuring the mob that they were to have their will. Without more ado, the three condemned men were dragged out of the Tolbooth and escorted through the wild throng who hurled insults and refuse at them and then fell in behind to form so closely packed a procession that it was said one could have walked on their heads all the way from Edinburgh to Leith. There the three Englishmen were hanged at the tidemark on the sands, the spot having been chosen by the authorities because the crime of which they had been found guilty was committed at sea.

The mood of Scotland changed suddenly when the men were pronounced dead. It was as if the whole people were overcome by the shame of what they had done. The mobs dissolved, the shouting ceased, and the remaining twelve convicted members of the *Worcester*'s crew were reprieved and in due course quietly freed with scarcely a word uttered anywhere in opposition. The anger rising through a century of insult and injury under the union of the crowns had erupted because it could be contained no longer. Something English had to be smashed and it was the cruellest of fates that brought the three sailors into the port of Leith at this time and made them that something.

Queen Anne's young Commissioner, the twenty-seven years old Duke of Argyll, was the son of the Earl of Argyll whom King William had made a duke for helping Queensberry to save the administration from Hamilton's onslaughts in the Darien debates. He had succeeded his father in September 1703 in the height of the agitation over the crown's rejection of the first Act of Security but had played no part in politics at that time, being too intent on making a military career under Marlborough in Flanders. His family held a unique position in the political history of Scotland. They headed the great Campbell clan of the west Highlands, tracing their ancestry into the mists of antiquity, and exercising lordship over vast acres of moor, mountain and loch, and all their inhabitants. For centuries they had regarded themselves as subordinate to no one whose superiority they did not choose to acknowledge. Other Highland grandees were no less proud and strongly contested the claims of the Campbells to the premier place among the clans, but none of them could rival the Campbells in the prestige which the family had built up among the lowland population of Scotland. All Highlanders were cattle-stealers and cut-purses to the lowlanders and their chiefs had to be specially able to rise above this reputation and play, as the Duke of Atholl had succeeded in doing, more than a minor military role in the affairs of their country. In the Highlands the Campbells were detested and feared as master-aggrandisers; in the lowlands they were numbered with the heroes and saints. Religion and two executions accounted for the anomaly.

The Campbells had been quick to embrace Protestantism during the Reformation, and when Charles I and Archbishop Laud sought to force the English prayer-book on the Kirk, Archibald, eighth Earl of Argyll, was a leading figure in the General Assembly which in 1638 defied the king and asserted the right of Scots to make their own Solemn Covenant with God and stay Presbyterians. Anxious to have the support of the clan if his disputes with Kirk and parliament should escalate into civil war, Charles forgave the earl and made him a marquess in 1641.

PLATE III

James Douglas,
4th Duke of Hamilton

James Douglas,
2nd Duke of Queensberry

James Ogilvy,
1st Earl of Seafield

Sidney Godolphin,
1st Earl of Godolphin

PLATE IV

John Campbell,
2nd Duke of Argyll

John Murray,
1st Duke of Atholl

Andrew Fletcher of Saltoun

John Hamilton, 2nd Lord Belhaven

Archibald took the bribe but was not to be bought. When the time came he took the field with the Scottish forces against Charles. However, when Charles was executed in 1649, it was Archibald Campbell, Marquess of Argyll, who with his own hand put the crown of Scotland on Charles II's head. When Cromwell overcame the Scots, Archibald made his peace with him, saving himself from exile and his estates from forfeiture. Charles II could not pardon such collaboration with the regicides, even in the man who had given him his first crown, and had him sequestered and beheaded in 1661. Presbyterian Scots had not forgotten Argyll's stand for the Kirk twenty-three years earlier and as the king earned their hatred by his heartless persecution of the Covenanters, so grew their respect and affection for the marquess, a martyred defender of their faith.

Archibald's son had not followed his father in co-operating with Cromwell but had kept up the struggle in the Highlands until Charles, from his exile in Holland, ordered him to lay down his arms. Three years after his father's execution Charles restored the estates and the earldom to the son. It was not long, however, before the family sympathy with the Covenanters brought him also into trouble. He was charged with having made reservations in his oath of allegiance to the king and condemned to death, but he escaped from Edinburgh Castle disguised as a lady's page and took refuge in Holland. When James II succeeded Charles, he returned to Scotland and tried to raise a Presbyterian army to push the Catholic off the throne. He was insufficiently supported even by his own clan, was captured by the Marquess of Atholl (as related in the previous chapter) and carried to Edinburgh where he was executed without trial in June 1685. 'Thus fell this great man,' writes Robert Campbell in his account of the family published in 1745, 'a martyr to the religion and liberty of his native country, whose merit and faithful service both to his country and the ungrateful House of Stuart deserved a better fate.'

The double martyrdom raised the Campbells of Argyll to an almost legendary stature among the Covenanters and, indeed, the whole lowland membership of the Kirk. The Highland origin and base of the family were forgotten or ignored. They were born of a long line of noble Scottish ancestors, had owned wealth and power, and went to the block for Scotland and the Scottish faith. This was the stuff of which ballads could be made. The Presby-

D

terians made it into sermons and the Argyll name was invoked when preachers thought the faith was weakening or being challenged.

The new Commissioner, John Campbell, second Duke of Argyll, had been seven years old when his grandfather was beheaded by James. His eighteenth-century biographer, the Robert Campbell already mentioned, records that at the moment of the execution the boy fell out of a window three storeys up in the house of his aunt without being hurt, and the superstitious believed this meant that 'this noble infant, miraculously preserved, would one day recover the lustre of the family of Argyll, then in a manner extinct by the barbarous murder and forfeiture of the earl.' His father did not wait for the lustre to be recovered by the son. Escaping to Holland and returning with William of Orange in 1688, he was one of three noblemen deputed to offer the Scottish crown to the Dutch prince and administer the coronation oath. He was sworn a Privy Councillor and soon afterwards was made a lord of the treasury and colonel of the Scots Guards. When the Treaty of Ryswick in 1697 temporarily ended the war with France, he took his seat in parliament and four years later, as we have seen, his family and personal prestige helped Queensberry to gather a majority and weather the post-Darien storm whipped up by the Duke of Hamilton. He enjoyed his elevation to a dukedom for only two years.

Although only twenty-five years old when he succeeded to the title, the new duke was already a seasoned soldier and well on the way to high command in the army. 'His capacity was equal to the most abstracted science,' writes respectful Robert Campbell, 'but, having a high spirit, and soon taking a liking to the army, he could not be prevailed upon to give much application to books but bent his whole attention to that science wherein he afterwards made so great a figure. . . . His father, perceiving that his son's genius was entirely turned to the military, encouraged it as the most likely course to recover the sinking state of the family.' The 'sinking state', Robert is referring to was the financial ability of the Campbells to sustain their status in the style expected of them. 'The troubles of his last two predecessors,' he remarks, speaking of the first duke's death, 'and his own expense, obliged him to leave the estate of Argyll pretty much involved.' He hints at what he means by 'his own expense'. 'The greatest crime his most avowed enemies charged him with was a more than ordinary fondness for the fair sex, a foible which is frequently met with in the greatest men, and from which few of his family were free.' The first duke may not have spent very much money on women, however, a foible which would not have gone unnoticed by the Kirk; another explanation for his debts is also offered by Robert. He was, he says, a man of great capacity but 'he wanted that application to business which distinguished his ancestors'. He had not, at least, collected so many salaried government posts to swell the income from his estates as Queensberry.

There was no doubt of the son's application to his chosen business. Thanks to his father's influence with King William, he started off in 1694 in command of a regiment of foot at the age of seventeen and lost no opportunity in the Flanders campaign of demonstrating that he had the capacity for leadership and the courage and enterprise which might have been expected from one of his ancestry. In the year before he succeeded to the title he had particularly distinguished himself by his gallantry at the capture of Keyserwaert, and, as he obviously stood high in the estimation of Marlborough, generalissimo of the allied armies since the death of William, his future as a soldier seemed assured. On his succession Queen Anne made him a Privy Councillor, colonel of the horse guards in Scotland, and a Knight of the Thistle, an order which she revived to placate her nobler Scottish subjects for whom there was no room in the Order of the Garter. Promoted brigadier-general, Argyll had commanded a division at Blenheim. John Macky, whose opinion of him is likely to be more candid than Robert Campbell's, wrote of him at the time: 'His family will not lose in his person the great figure they have made for so many ages in that kingdom, having all the free spirits and good sense natural to the family. Few of his years have a better understanding, nor a more manly behaviour. He hath seen most of the courts of Europe, is very handsome in appearance, fair-complexioned.' It was not difficult to see why Anne and Godolphin, when they decided that the feeble Squadrone Volante government had to be reinforced or replaced, should turn to the young Duke of Argyll and put him in the key post of Lord High Commissioner. He was completely inexperienced in politics but he had several advantages: the family reputation as champions of Scotland and the Kirk would ensure him of popular support; that reputation, enhanced by his forthright manner and the gift of oratory he had begun to display, would counter-balance the appeal of Hamilton in parliament and the country; he was a fighter and would not be pushed off course as Tweeddale had been; he was trusted by the Whigs in the English parliament, as a soldier who had campaigned under William and Marlborough, and as a member of a family who had demonstrated their belief in the right of the landed interest over the disposal of the crown; and, his heart being set on military glory, he would stand apart from the politicians and might be able to bring the more important of them together to form a pro-government majority because they would have no need to fear him as a rival for political place and power. Godolphin hoped he might even be able to effect a rapprochement with Queensberry. His close acquaintances had no doubt of his courage and strength of will. Some feared that his outbursts of pride, his impatience with anything that thwarted him, and the heat of his temper when his emotions were roused, were handicaps which his habitual grace of manner and generally cheerful disposition might not wholly overcome. But they were agreed that he was honest, incapable of deceit, the last person to be overawed by power or influenced by favour and that that should commend him to Scots in their present mood. Anne took a little persuasion; she disliked him as a Whig and found him more outspoken than she preferred her subjects to be. There was no question, however, of his loyalty to her army, her Marlborough, her war, and therefore to her England and her crown. So, if Godolphin said he was the man, she was prepared to accept him.

The murders of Green, Mather and Simpson had purged the unbearable fire from the bellies of the Scots but the resentment, the hatred, and the problem remained. The *Worcester* affair had been the tempestuous rampage of a drunk and now the nation faced the morning after. Nothing had changed or been added except the disgrace they had brought upon themselves. Christmas Day was eight short months away and in that time they had to decide what they were to do about the ultimatum of the English Alien Act. Were they to knuckle down to tame acceptance of the House of Hanover on the English terms, or keep their pride and be crushed to an even lower level of poverty and degradation, or smash out again, alone or with any help that was offered?

Although a soldier and a fighter, the young Duke of Argyll rejected a resort to arms. He had no desire to fight the English, with whom he got along very well, and the last thing he wanted was to become involved with the Jacobites in any venture that might bring a more intractable Stuart than Anne to the throne of either country. He supported the Hanover succession but was realist enough to know that it was no longer acceptable to the Scots without considerable amendment of the union in their favour. He felt sure that if the matter were handled properly a new union could be negotiated. The temperature had to be brought down first, which meant persuading the English parliament to repeal the Alien Act before Christmas. This in turn made it essential that there should be a government in Scotland which was capable of convincing the English that a reconciliatory gesture on their part would be followed speedily and without fail by firm embrace of Hanover. A more experienced politician might have quailed at the task of mollifying a public opinion as outraged as that of the Scots when intriguers and orators like Hamilton and Atholl were bent on aggravating it. Argyll had the optimism of youth and the self-confidence of a Highland aristocrat whose whistle brought clansmen to his heels as easily as dogs. He was too astute, however, to attempt the job alone. It could be done, he believed, with two men at his side – Queensberry, the ablest politician in Scotland, and Seafield, the anchor-man of every political combination.

He had first to remove the Marquess of Tweeddale and his Squadrone Volante government and then separate Queensberry from his allies of the previous summer, Atholl and Hamilton. Anne could not demur at dismissing Tweeddale and his fellow-ministers. Their behaviour in the *Worcester* affair had been unforgiveable – skulking in their country houses or in pretended sick-beds and leaving all the burden to be carried by poor Seafield. Even the mob they were dodging found them contemptible. Their dismissal also helped to placate those English who wanted retribution for the murder of Green, Mather and Simpson. She accepted Queensberry on the argument that only he could now save the union from total disruption. Argyll had no difficulty in putting the argument to Queensberry. He had joined up with Atholl and Hamilton and organised the passing of the Act of Security to win back the public favour he had lost through falling for Simon

Fraser's lies, to punish Anne and Godolphin for dropping him, and to demonstrate his political mastery. All this he had accomplished. Who, having marched the Scots to the top of the hill, was in a better position to talk them into following him down again? Queensberry had never been an anti-union man, he hated Atholl, and he had no confidence in Hamilton. Nobody had expected him to find them comfortable political bed-fellows, not even the dukes themselves. There was no great surprise, therefore, when it was announced that he had deserted the opposition and accepted office in a new government as Lord Privy Seal. Seafield needed no persuasion. He shared the general view that no government, wherever it might be heading, could be complete without him.

The members of the Scottish parliament assembled in Edinburgh at the end of June with a full sense of the momentousness of the session about to begin. They all knew it had to be make or break before Christmas. The question was: could any way be found to make when all the winds were howling for breaking?

6 The Battle of the Dukes

Never before in the history of Edinburgh had there been so much debate in and around the Parliament House as there was that summer. Never before had what might be decided in it seemed so important to its members. Never before had a Scots parliament felt the attention of the nation, and indeed of Europe, to be concentrated on its deliberations.

The issue that had to be settled in this single session was of vital importance, not only to the Scots and the English, but also to most of the governments of Europe and to all those parts of the earth in which English, French, Spaniards and Dutch were settling or trading, for on it could hang whether England was to be strengthened or weakened in the power struggle with France. For the first time since the last quarter of Elizabeth's reign Scotland was back on the international map and for the first time the members of its legislative assembly could feel that the determination of its future was truly in their hands and had not already been decided for them by king or privy council. For the first time they were bearing the heavy responsibility of representative government.

Of the three hundred and fifteen nobles and commoners who made up the membership only a handful had any clear idea of how they wanted the debating to go.

Among these were the members of the new ministry headed by Argyll, Queensberry and Seafield. They sought no more out of the session than authority for the appointment of commissioners to negotiate with the English for better terms of union, and hoped that if they got this far Godolphin and Wharton could persuade the English parliament to repeal the Alien Act before it came into force at Christmas. They had ideas about where the better terms of union should lead but they were saying little about them for the moment. The tactic they had decided on was one of gradualism;

the first step should be open-ended negotiation with no prior commitment to anything.

Apparently equally clear-minded in their determination to frustrate negotiation were Atholl and Hamilton and a small number of members who openly avowed attachment to the Jacobite cause. It was enough for their purpose if nothing at all happened in this session and the Alien Act came into operation. That would guarantee a rapid heightening of the tensions between Scotland and England, make it impossible for the Scots to accept the House of Hanover, and leave the way open for James Stuart to come over from France whenever the time seemed ripe.

The immediate objectives of both the government and the opposition leaders were strictly limited, therefore, and in neither case opened any windows on a visible future for Scotland, except that the government leaned to Hanover and the opposition to Stuart. The numbers of firm adherents on both sides were few and evenly balanced at the commencement of the session.

The great bulk of the members milled around in a fog of conflicting emotions and convictions, united only by their outraged nationalism. It also divided them. A member could inveigh against the English in a tavern and see no way out but war, and he would rouse the hackles of all around him until they began asking themselves what were his motives. Did he want war simply to vent his just rage or to compel the English to give Scots freedom of trade? Was it to burst the union wide apart or force it closer? Was it to win England for James and perhaps the French? If it was the first or the second they could all cry aye with him until the bottle was empty. If it was total severance he was after, however, they would have to part from him if they had any interests in or hopes from free trade. If it was closer union, they had to ask him under what king and what parliament. If Hanover, that might be all right if his hearers were Presbyterians, or even Episcopalians, but not if they were crypto-Catholics or for some other reason were inclined to the Stuarts. Did he want Scotland to keep its parliament or to surrender everything to Westminster? Did he realise that one parliament in Westminster would ring the death-knell of the Presbyterian Kirk? Perhaps that was his real motive. Perhaps as an Episcopalian he wanted all to be slaves to the Archbishop of Canterbury, or as a Catholic to the Pope of Rome. If he professed Presbyterianism and wanted to put James on the

throne, what guarantees could he offer of a future for the
Protestant religion and the Kirk? Could any war with England
be won without the French? Would the French come in without
James, without the Pope? And if the war was lost – remember
Marlborough! – what would happen then? Another Cromwell,
English garrisons, no parliament and no Kirk? The argument
went noisily and endlessly round and round in the taverns in the
first weeks of the session.

In more sober discussions there was the same division and
questions, the same difficulty in finding any solution on which
most men were likely to agree. The larger number in Parliament
House were convinced Presbyterians. The dominant influence on
their thinking, in addition to their own welfare, was the security
of the Kirk. That suggested preference for the Hanover succession,
which was intended to preserve Protestantism in England, but
many hesitated to embrace it. The commonest objection was that
Hanover was an English choice and would perpetuate rule from
London in the English interest with all the evils which that was
producing. This was reinforced in many cases by a lingering senti-
ment for the direct male line of the Stuarts in spite of all the perils
to which they had subjected the Kirk. James was a shade closer to
being Scots than his German cousins, could perhaps more easily
be persuaded to give a thought to Scotland than the Germans.
If he would only agree to become a Presbyterian, or at least a
Protestant of some kind, there need be no problem. This wishful
thinking could not go far, however, without coming up against
the union issue and the hard economics of the situation. Realists
among the Presbyterians were reluctant to face the prospect of
Scotland's going it alone. In their view the prime need was to make
the English agree to give Scots equal access with themselves
to all the economic opportunities of the whole island and all the
possessions and interests England was acquiring overseas. For this
a few were prepared to jettison James Stuart, accept Hanover,
and take risks with the security of the Kirk and the survival of
Scots nationhood. A larger number agreed that economics tipped
the balance against the Stuarts, but remained fearful of the risks
to Kirk and national institutions and traditions which were involved in closer union, if it were obtainable. These misgivings
brought some of the more nationalistic to accept Hanover as probably being the only means of securing the freedom of the Kirk

while opposing all talk of closer union. Between the pro-Hanover realists and the pro-Hanover nationalists was still another group of Presbyterians who were ready to have Hanover for the Kirk and union for the trade, but debated what degree of union. Could they be accepted as trading partners by the English and yet avoid being integrated with them? Among these Andrew Fletcher of Saltoun was pressing his solution: union but with limitations, a loose federation in which there could be mutuality of trade and defence but otherwise everything would stay separate and wholly independent. They could have one king or none, for all he cared, so long as they kept out the Stuarts.

It was on this confused crowd of Presbyterians that Argyll, Queensberry and Seafield had to depend for a majority. They had to assure the disquieted that they had nothing to fear from entering into negotiation with the English and to encourage all those who favoured or feared a particular approach or outcome to believe that negotiating offered the best way to promote it or kill it. There were some things of which they were themselves sure. One was that the English would not be content with anything short of a single king and government for the whole island. This they now knew to be essential to their security and if they could not get it by negotiation they would enforce it by war. Another was that the English would not want to go to war with Scotland, at least so long as they were menaced by the French. Scotland could negotiate, therefore, from a position that had a measure of strength. The blackmail that had persuaded Godolphin to advise Anne to approve the Act of Security could still be worked. The question was the price the English would be prepared to pay in trade and concessions to Scottish national pride to buy their safety. It was in this area only that the negotiations could be open-ended, as Argyll, Queensberry and Seafield well knew. But there was little of this they could say to the supporters they had to woo without scaring some and making fierce opponents out of others, without danger of being forced into commitments which would cut down the negotiating options, perhaps completely hamstring the negotiations before they began, and without giving openings to the opposition which they would not hesitate to use to leave the triumvirate powerless to get anything at all through. It was as tricky a situation as any government ever faced.

Atholl and Hamilton were fully aware of the problems that

the government front bench faced. They blew on the fires of animosity against the English, terrified Presbyterians with tales of the fate of the Kirk under the High Tories, threatened lawyers with the loss of their learning and fees when closer union brought English law into Scotland as it assuredly would, and alarmed all and sundry with the dangers to their pockets, their privileges and perquisites, their status, manners, speech and customs if the border barriers were lowered and the English tax-gatherers, excise-men, judges, justices of the peace, and the whole paraphernalia of the alien southern system were invited to move in. It was little help for Presbyterian realists to counter by arguing that all these calamities were more certain to fall on the country if the Scots went to war with the English or the English were forced to go to war with them and that the best course was to negotiate and give away as little as possible for as much as possible. Lowland lairds and Highland chiefs who stood too much on their dignity or had too little capital or intelligence to fancy themselves as successful speculators in English or other markets could see no reason why they should go out of their way to risk the substance they enjoyed, meagre though it might be, to aid meaner folks' dreams of being their equals or betters. If any were tempted, opposition advocates were soon around to argue that commerce with the French and their colonies could be as lucrative as England's, involved far less risk to the Scottish way of life because the French were well across the water, and in any case the auld alliance made the Scots and the French more congenial to one another than ever Scots and English could be. In the prevailing mood, and among people so many of whom were connected with France by birth, education or service over a couple of generations or more, the argument carried weight. As for the Kirk, was it in any more danger from an association with the French than it would be from union with the English? Louis might have persecuted the Huguenots, but were Presbyterians and other dissenters not denied citizenship rights in England? The anti-negotiatiors could easily bemuse a man, drunk or sober.

Probing the motivation of the ducal contenders was equally contentious. Nobody could question the loyalty of the Duke of Argyll to the Kirk but it was possible to sow doubts about him in other respects. He was young, a Campbell, which made him obnoxious to other Highlanders, and probably ambitious to improve on the power and comparative wealth which his family had acquired. He had served under Marlborough and had very influential friends in London. Here he was, at twenty-seven, the queen's Commissioner, holding the major office in Scotland in the gift of the London politicians. He was well-placed to look after his own interests in any merger of Scotland into England and no doubt considered that, so far as he was personally concerned, any losses would be more than balanced by his gains. He could not pretend to be a disinterested pleader for negotiation towards a closer union. It was possible, if one leant that way, to see him as an honest and honourable man who would regard it as his duty to fight hard for Scotland in these negotiations. If there were no alternative to negotiation, he might be a good man to lead Scotland into it. The nagging doubt remained, nevertheless, that when it came to a choice he might subserve the national to his personal interest.

The same, and more, applied to the Duke of Queensberry. He had been on the best of terms with all the powers in London for a much longer time than Argyll. True, he had recently been out of favour and had led the revolt over the Act of Security, but here he was back again promoting conciliation with the English – surely an indication that power and place meant more to him than principle, and that his leadership of the opposition in the previous summer had been nothing more than a bid to hold popular esteem and show the London politicians that they could not do without him. It was possible to believe that he was following a calculated policy in the interests of Scotland, that he had seen the Act of Security as a necessary step to force the English to take his country's claims to better union terms seriously, was now bent on getting all he could by negotiation, but would have no hesitation in leading revolt again if he failed to secure all he considered essential. One could go so far and still have doubts. Whatever Argyll gave away, it would not be the Kirk. Could the same reliance be placed on Queensberry? He was known to have a soft spot for Episcopalians. He would probably be a tough fighter for the economic benefits, the established law system and the like, but might not keep the doors barred against bishops.

Seafield? It was little use studying his predilections for he had none except for making a ship-shape job of whatever he had to turn his hand to. The only thing he would fight for was administrative tidiness and at this juncture who cared about that?

One duke there was no doubt about was Atholl. Everybody knew where he stood since his resignation over the Fraser scandal. He was wholeheartedly for James, and pressed the case without equivocation. Negotiation was anathema to him. So was union unless under James and the best way to secure it was to put James on the throne of Scotland and, with French help, dictate terms to England. The terms could include everything everybody wanted – trade, Kirk, law, institutions and privileges. Atholl was no great orator in the parliament chamber, and no match for Queensberry if the debate came down to facts and figures, but in lobbying his passionate vehemence could temporarily sweep away the qualms of any who had not been inoculated against Jacobitism by family denominational history or more recent political and economic conviction. He could turn haughty and imperious, however, if the argument didn't wholly go his way and so lost supporters he might have gained with more forebearance. He was more of a gadfly to the government than a real menace but he held the small band of convinced Jacobites firmly together, and the possibility of his taking less committed votes with him in any critical division could not be discounted.

If any man could have decided the issue by sheer weight of popular regard it was the Duke of Hamilton. As an acknowledged champion of the interests of Scotland he towered high above the other dukes. He was in the prime of life, and experienced, while Argyll was young. Queensberry had been the servitor of London. Hamilton had been the most vigorous spokesman of opposition to London. He had led the disgruntled Presbyterians when they found it necessary to stand up to William of Orange, had been the nation's voice in its dreams, rages and griefs over Darien, and, although Queensberry had manipulated the passage of the Act of Security, Hamilton had been its conceiver and public driving-force. There was no question of the purity of his nationalism, his adherence to the Kirk, and his immunity from suspicion of cherishing career or other aspirations for which he needed friends in England. The loftiness of his position seemed to put him above other men's ambitions. Most honourably descended from the Douglas who had been Bruce's right-hand, the blood royal flowed in his veins through the marriage of an ancestor to the sister of James III of Scotland. He was a man of the world, and, had been Charles II's ambassador-extraordinary to Versailles in his early twenties, aide-de-camp to Louis XIV, gentleman of the bedchamber and master of the wardrobe to James II, and had twice been thrown into the Tower by William of Orange. He was wealthy, with large estates in Scotland and, through his wife, in Staffordshire and Lancashire. He had the power of public oratory which Atholl lacked. If the Duke of Hamilton had been for union and negotiation there would have been no need for debate in Edinburgh that summer. A large majority of the members of parliament would willingly have followed him and been well content to leave it to him to get the best terms for everybody.

They all knew, of course, that he was implacably opposed to union and negotiation. If opposition pure and simple had been possible, a majority might also have been trustfully with him. But opposers had to be for something and, in so far as he had declared himself, Hamilton appeared to be leaning towards James, which was disconcerting to some. The difficulty was that no one was certain whom he wished to succeed to the throne. His pro- motion of the Act of Security settled nothing. Some of his talk suggested that he opposed Hanover because he definitely wanted to snatch the throne for James when Anne should die. At other times it seemed he might be merely threatening the English and would be ready to withdraw his opposition to union if the English gave way on trade. He was doing all he could to frustrate negotiation. Was that, perhaps, a tactic designed to postpone negotiations until he had convinced London that there was no alternative but to negotiate with himself and not Argyll and Queensberry? Was the inclination towards James, and the trafficking with the Courts of St Germains and Versailles, which he did not deny, a part of that tactic, or was he, like many others on both sides of the border, merely keeping his options open, but, unlike most of these, with the good of Scotland in mind and not his own? It was possible to give him the benefit of the doubt if one was reluctant to abandon his leadership.

Disturbing questions were asked by the government side in their efforts to counter his influence. He had voluntarily stayed on in France when his mission to Louis was completed and fought two campaigns in the close personal entourage of that Grand Catholic Monarch. Was it not Louis who had pressed him on

James II in the intimate office of gentleman of the bedchamber and master of the wardrobe? Why had the champion of Protestantism, William of Orange, thought it necessary to commit him twice to the Tower? Why had a warrant been issued against him after he returned to Scotland? Was he not buying votes in certain quarters with money sent him by Louis and the Pope? No good Presbyterian could wholly dismiss these sinister insinuations. The duke might not, however, be as black as they were trying to paint him. Why had he been released from the Tower and why had he not been tried on that Scottish warrant of arrest? Had his father not been William of Orange's first Commissioner in Scotland and on his death had not William granted his widow's request that the ducal title and lands which were hers by inheritance be transferred to her son without waiting for her death? Could that have happened under Protestant William if there had been any real reason to suspect the son of conspiring with the enemies of Protestantism? As for buying votes, the government had no scruples about buying them when they had the wherewithal and Hamilton might be putting the French and papal money to a sound Scottish national purpose. Opinion see-sawed with the complexion of the company.

Another thought was aired. Perhaps the duke was not altogether beyond the reached of personal ambition. There was that matter of his royal descent. Might it be that he was interested in furthering the cause neither of James nor Sophia of Hanover but his own? If Scotland were separated conclusively from England and the House of Hanover, and if Presbyterian prejudice and the fear of England restrained any considerable body of Scots from calling in James Stuart, it was not inconceivable that they could be prompted to turn to King James Douglas, the idol of the populace and ready to hand. If one were disposed to credit the suggestion, it offered a plausible explanation of some puzzling things in the duke's relations with the Jacobites. If he were for James, why had he never responded to any of the pressures the agents of the Court of St Germains were known to have put on him to raise the standard of revolt? There had been occasions when, in their view at least, he could have done so with a prospect of success. There was the fact too, evident to the sharp-eyed, that while he was *with* Atholl and the more rabid Jacobites he was not *of* them. It was said by some who claimed to be in the

know that St Germains had dropped him and was taking it ill
that Versailles continued to finance him. Louis might be looking
on him as a more likely pretender than James. It could all be
made to add up to something. However, it did not follow that the
government could count on the votes of all who were doing
the arithmetic. Presbyterian nationalists who shied away from
Hanover for fear of subservience to England and from the Stuarts
for fear of Catholicism might not be averse to considering how
the crown would look on a Douglas head. It was an interesting
extension of the circle of candidates and need not deter members
from voting with Hamilton if they were inclined to see eye to eye
with him for other reasons. Even the confirmed Jacobites could
not afford to quarrel with him in any of his oppositions – Hanover,
union or negotiation.

The contest in the chamber was formally opened by the Earl
of Mar, who moved on behalf of the government that parliament
should authorise the appointment of commissioners to treat with
England for an amended union in accordance with the letter
and spirit of the Act of Security. Although only thirty and less
than ten years in politics, Mar was already earning the nickname
of 'Bobbing John' which was to become firmly fixed on him by
1715, when, spurned by George I, he fled in pique back to
Scotland and raised the standard for the Pretender. His family
had been severely hit by fines and sequestration in the political
vicissitudes of the previous half-century and Mar was so burdened
with debt when he succeeded to the title in 1696 that he had to
look for political protectors to save him from his creditors. Friends
in the government kept him out of their clutches and in return he
became a firm supporter of the court party in parliament,
and particularly of Queensberry, an association which had
continued until Queensberry was brought down by the Fraser
plot and succeeded by Tweeddale and the Squadrone Volante.
Mar had no friends in the Squadrone government and, when
Queensberry joined Hamilton in opposition, he flirted discreetly
with the other opposition group, the Jacobites. According to
Lockhart, he did it 'with so much art and dissimulation that he
gained the favour of all the Tories, and was by many of them
esteemed an honest man, and well inclined to the royal family.'
His art had also kept him in with Queensberry, however, and

when that duke returned to office with Argyll to secure Scotland for Hanover, he had shown no hesitation in joining them and abandoning St Germains. There was a touch of cynicism, therefore, in choosing him to move for negotiation with the English. He had a hump-back, and little more than a smooth tongue to help him overcome the handicap. He had no popularity with the Country Party and was now totally out of favour with the Jacobites. The government could not have hoped for anything from an opening speech by him, however persuasive. They may have merely been using him to test the temperature of the water. No support for his motion came from anywhere but the government front bench. Speaker after speaker rose to protest that before any negotiations could be started parliament must decide what the commissioners were to negotiate about.

None of the dukes had any desire for an immediate head-on collision. Both government and opposition wanted the members to talk themselves into realising that they would never reach agreement. Argyll and Queensberry hoped that sheer weariness would persuade a majority to nod in the end for negotiation, as the only way of getting a respite from the agonies of decision. Hamilton and Atholl were confident that they could stoke fear and frustration into a final explosive no. Since the members were obviously not yet ready to commit themselves to James Stuart, and since King James Douglas was only a background whisper, they launched into a protracted wrangle over Hanover. Queensberry said all there was to be said for the Hanoverian succession. Hamilton paraded the dangers to nation and Kirk and the impossibility of accepting dictates under duress. Andrew Fletcher of Saltoun had his day – quite a few days, in fact.

He was the first purely secular social and political revolutionary to emerge in Scotland. Son of a landed proprietor in the Lothians, he was marked as a firebrand in his twenties for opposing the Duke of Lauderdale's efforts to raise forces to intimidate the Covenanters. He had been compelled to board and lodge soldiers at his own expense as a punishment and had fled to Brussels, whence the English ambassador reported of him: 'Here is one Fletcher, laird of Saltoun, lately come from Scotland. He is an ingenious but a violent fanatic, and doubtless has some commission, for I hear he is very busy and virulent.' The business was helping Monmouth to try to overthrow James II. He took part in Monmouth's invasion of the west of England and was saved from death or capture at Sedgmoor by his uncontrollable temper. Disagreeing with the Taunton alderman who was Monmouth's local guide, he shot him dead, contributing to the mishaps that led to the expedition's defeat. Monmouth let him flee to Bilbao where he was arrested. He escaped and wandered through Spain and eventually into Hungary where he fought against the Turks. He was tried for treason at Edinburgh in his absence and sentenced to death and forfeiture of his estate. When he returned with William of Orange, his revolutionary fervour had not abated, although parliament passed a special act to give him back his estate. He tried to found a 'Young Scotland' movement and a home-rule party and published treatises in which he advocated setting up camps for military training of the young, free of religious influence, and also the diversion of the money spent on regular troops in Scotland to the promotion of industry. An odd-sounding proposal for a man of his outlook was that Scotland's numerous beggars and vagrants should be compelled to enter the service of landowners, who would be at liberty to buy and sell their offspring but not to call them slaves! He enthusiastically supported William Paterson's Darien scheme and subscribed a thousand pounds.

A member of the Country Party, he had moved the Act anent Peace and War which forbade the queen to commit Scotland to war without parliament's consent. He had also moved without success his own version of the Act of Security under which Scotland was to have home rule, annual parliaments, ministers appointed by a committee of M.P.s and not by the crown, a national militia, and for every new Scottish peer a balancing commoner to be added to the membership of parliament. His latest published work had been *An Account of a Conversation concerning the Right Regulation of Governments for the Common Good of Mankind*, in which he had made the often quoted declaration that if he were given the making of a nation's songs he cared not who made its laws. Macky, to whom he was a dangerous radical, pictures him as 'a low, thin man, brown complexion, full of fire, with a stern, sour look.' Lockhart, more admiringly, declares he was 'so steadfast to what he thought right that no hazard nor advantage, no, not the universal empire, nor the gold of America, could tempt him to yield or desert it.'

He was so determined to use the current debate to turn Scotland, if not into the independent republic he longed for, at least into a self-governing entity, free of English control and as democratic as a landowner of his day could conceive, that he paid scant attention to the rulings of the chair and was ready to challenge to a duel members of the government or his own party who denied him what he considered a fair hearing.

He supported Hanover but with limitations clearly defined and constitutionally enshrined to keep the crown in London merely as a symbol of an association of the kingdoms, and with no power in Scotland other than a Scots parliament might give it. He advocated union in so far as it could be operated while leaving Scotland in full control of all her own internal affairs and he proposed negotiation thus far but definitely no farther. This form of federal union for which he was pleading seemed to him to provide the ideal solution for everybody but Atholl and the Jacobites, and he had no use for them. With support from any of the other three dukes, Fletcher might have had a majority of the House behind him. But Argyll and Queensberry were opposed to negotiation with such limitations, for the good reason that they knew the English had already decided that federal union was insufficient to meet their defensive needs and would certainly never barter any worthwhile trade concessions for it. Hamilton was against the scheme because it involved Hanover and negotiation. Fletcher was a dogged fighter and had done his homework. He had them consider every country where there was or ever had been any form of federation – the ancient and mediaeval worlds, Switzerland, Holland, Poland, Spain and Portugal – but for every merit he could list his opponents produced a telling flaw in the management of these nations. Eventually his proposals were turned down and after some more desultory debate the House decided not to commit itself as yet to Hanover. The fruitless discussions continued for eight weeks in all.

However, an important piece of manoeuvring had been effected behind the scenes. One of the problems of Argyll and Queensberry was the votes of the twenty-odd members of the Squadrone Volante, who had formed the inept government of the previous summer, trounced by Hamilton and Queensberry and dismissed by Argyll. Since the session began they had done little but sulk and lick their wounds. If they kept up their grudge against the government dukes, their own votes might give victory to the opposition and waverers might take a lead from them. On the other hand they could not be feeling very partial to Hamilton and when in office they had been pro-Hanover and union. Some of them had ambitions but were calculating rather than adventurous and were susceptible to the inducements of patronage which Argyll and Queensberry could hold out to them. Seafield, who had been a member of their ministry, was set to work on them and towards the end of August he reported that he had won them over. It was decided to put Mar's motion for negotiation to the test again.

It was re-introduced on the last day of August. Many members were obviously sick of debate and Hamilton was afraid to risk a straight negative to the motion for negotiation. He tried a wrecking tactic. He moved that the negotiators be prohibited from entering into any agreement which would destroy or depreciate any of the fundamental laws, ancient privileges, rights, dignities, liberties and institutions of the kingdom of Scotland. It was a glorious patriotic catch-all of an addendum, the direct antithesis of the untrammelled negotiation the government sought, aimed at appealing to every fear and prejudice and sinking the negotiations before they had begun.

Until the very last votes were cast it was touch and go that he would succeed. The amendment was defeated by two.

The front bench was relieved but not elated. They knew the battle was not yet over. Next morning Hamilton played what he believed was a trump card. He moved that negotiations should not begin until the English had withdrawn their ultimatum and repealed the threatening Alien Act. Passionately he renewed the argument that Scotland could not negotiate under duress. It would be forcing the nation to crawl on its knees to the English. Members had been subjected to remonstrance and abuse from angry patriots in the taverns overnight and many were having second thoughts about their yesterday's votes for negotiation. They could not take them back but Hamilton's motion offered a means of tying a string to them which could repair the damage they had done to their reputations as upholders of Scotland's pride and dignity. Queensberry had anticipated the move and countered it with a clever side-tracking proposal. He argued that tacking such a condition to the negotiation offer would not only have the effect of locking the Scottish and English parliaments in the unbreakable contest of wills which the Duke of Hamilton intended, but it would expose the Scottish parliament to the ridicule of the world for crying forward in one breath and back with the next. A more sensible procedure, he suggested, would be to let the negotiation motion stand as it was and approve a separate address to the queen informing her that, whatever negotiation might produce, nothing could be implemented until the unfriendly English Act had been expunged from the statute book. It was a masterly stroke which left Hamilton disarmed. Only the Jacobites put up any real opposition. Hamilton clenched his fists and cursed aloud.

Argyll and Queensberry had one more obstacle to overcome: the method by which the negotiating commissioners were to be appointed. They wanted to leave it to the queen, which meant that she would appoint on their advice and they could ensure that the nominees were balanced to their liking. Hamilton had declared he would insist on election by parliament and the government was very much afraid he would get his way. Opponents of union regarded this as their last stand. If they got enough of themselves elected to the commission they could still win back all the ground they had lost on the previous day. In desperation Argyll had approached Hamilton and offered to make a bargain with him. If Hamilton would agree to the queen's making the appointments Argyll would give his bond that Hamilton would be a commissioner. It was a feeble effort since, if the choice were decided by election, Hamilton knew he could be certain of a seat at the negotiating table, and it had been rejected with scorn.

Members had generally understood that the matter would not be raised that day, and when the address to the queen had been agreed most of the opposition took the opportunity of an early night after the long debates of the previous weeks, and left the chamber. Hamilton remained, apparently still stunned by the effectiveness of Queensberry's manoeuvre, and sat in gloomy silence through some routine business which the half-empty House proceeded to put through. When it had been completed he suddenly rose and to everybody's stupefaction blandly moved in his loftiest manner that the queen should appoint the commissioners, to avoid, as he put it, the heats and feuds in which they would all be plunged if election were adopted. When they had recovered from their astonishment at his amazing change of front the union opponents still in the chamber roared out their protests at the motion and the crime of proposing it at such a time. Dazed as he was at the inexplicable gift his adversary was handing him, Queensberry did not let his chance go. The vote was taken before the opposition could collect its wits and reinforcements and Hamilton's extraordinary motion was carried.

So, in a collapse of surprise, relief, rage and bewilderment, ended the chief business of a momentous session. Argyll and Queensberry had got what they wanted, but there was no joy anywhere. The ministers had done no more than scrape the first hurdle and knew it. Atholl was furious, Hamilton mum. Nothing had changed for the members of parliament except that they had astonished themselves by agreeing that some of them should go and knock on England's door. Most of them still did not know what kind of reception they ought to hope for or what their delegates would or should say if they were admitted. They went back to retracing the same old maze of argument they had dizzied themselves with for the last two months.

The only new topic was the shattering defection of Hamilton. Why had he done it? Was he a turncoat, had he been bought or intimidated, had he lost his nerve in the critical moment, or was it a subterfuge to deceive the other dukes, accept their rumoured guarantee of a place among the negotiators and use it Trojan-horse-like to ensure that all their schemes were brought to naught? More puzzling alleys had been added to the maze and more gloom to the outlook if the only result of all the deliberating was that they had lost a leader.

None of what had happened in parliament altered the mood of the country. Their betters might delude themselves with negotiation. The mass of the people knew, as they had always known, that nothing good for Scotland could be expected from the English.

7 A Treaty is Signed

While the Scots parliament had been screwing itself up to approach the English, Godolphin and the Whig allies who had kept him in office had put themselves in a better posture to receive the negotiators. In the summer of 1705 they had staged a general election and routed Godolphin's High Tory enemies. They had secured a mandate for Marlborough to go on and defeat Louis and confirmed that a large majority of the English electorate were behind them in their partiality for Hanover. Relations with Scotland had been overshadowed by the major issues in the election but its result had broken the power of the High Church, anti-Presbyterian and anti-Scottish element in the Tory party to frustrate the new government's intention of finding a speedy solution to the Anglo-Scottish problem.

Godolphin moved quickly. Within a few weeks of the Scots agreeing to negotiate, Anne requested the English parliament to repeal the Alien Act, and before November was out the Christmas ultimatum had been withdrawn 'to the end that the good and friendly disposition of this Kingdom towards the Kingdom of Scotland may appear.' The government declared its policy to be, in the words of Defoe, that 'to gain of the Scots what they ought to grant, it was reasonable to grant the Scots what they ought to have.' An act was passed empowering the queen to appoint commissioners to meet the Scots. Protests from the business community met with the firm response that the safety of the realm demanded a change of attitude towards the needy Scots.

Desperate to bring Godolphin and the Whigs down before they could achieve their end, the High Tories laid a cunning political trap. It was well known that, although Anne had accepted the idea of being succeeded by the Electress Sophia of Hanover or her son, she was bitterly jealous of court being paid to them by any of her subjects and had stubbornly rejected suggestions that the septuagenarian Sophia should be invited to visit her. There was consternation therefore on the government side when Lord Haversham moved in the Lords that Sophia be invited to take up residence in England until Anne's death, and was supported by the High Tory leaders who had hitherto strongly opposed Hanover. The reasons for the turnabout were obvious. High Tories were revenging themselves on Anne for going over with Godolphin to the Whigs and they were aiming to have Sophia on their side if and when they had to accept her. They were also putting the government in a most embarrassing position. If Godolphin agreed to the proposal, Anne, who could not bear the thought of Sophia in a rival court in London, would summarily dismiss him. If he opposed it, he would lose the favour he now enjoyed in Hanover and the support of all those who had voted for Hanover in the recent election. It looked at first as though Godolphin could not escape the pincers the High Tories had exchanged for their unsuccessful bludgeons of the previous year. Once again he was saved by the wily Wharton, who brought forward, as an alternative to the Haversham proposal, a Regency Bill to safeguard the Hanover succession against a snap move when Anne died: neither the Privy Council nor parliament would dissolve on Anne's death as had been customary, but would continue to function until her successor had been proclaimed, and had come over from Hanover, under a Council of Regency consisting of the Archbishop of Canterbury, the Lord Keeper of the Great Seal, the Lord Treasurer (Godolphin) and a number of other dignitaries. This adroit move cut the ground from under the High Tories. It provided all Hanover could ask for, pleased the voters, and made the Haversham motion a needless offence to the queen which parliament had no difficulty in finding superfluous. A final High Tory thrust at Godolphin – a motion to replace him in the Council of Regency by the Lord Mayor of London – was rejected, and danger from the enemies of the Scots was averted for the life of that parliament.

In February 1706 the queen announced the names of the commissioners she had appointed to negotiate for Scotland. There were thirty-one of them, fourteen peers and seventeen commoners. The peers were Queensberry, Seafield, the Earls of Mar, Loudon, Stair, Rosebery, Sutherland, Morton, Wemyss, Leven and

Glasgow, Viscount Dupplin, Lord Ross, and Lord Archibald
Campbell (brother of the Duke of Argyll), and the commoners
Sir Hugh Dalrymple (Lord President of the Court of Session),
Adam Cockburn of Ormiston (Lord Justice Clerk), Robert Dundas
of Arnistoun, Robert Stuart of Tillicoultry, Sir Alexander Ogilvy
of Forglen (Lords of Session), Francis Montgomery of Giffen, Sir
Patrick Johnston (provost of Edinburgh), Sir David Dalrymple,
Sir James Smollett, George Lockhart of Carnwath, William
Morison of Prestongrange, Alexander Grant the Younger, William
Seton the Younger of Pitmedden, John Clerk the Younger of
Pennycuick, Hugh Montgomery (provost of Glasgow) and Daniel
Campbell and Daniel Stuart (tax experts). All but one were, as
had been expected, supporters of closer union. There were two
surprises. The real surprise was that there was only one duke –
Queensberry. Argyll and Hamilton were missing. The other sur-
prise – to himself as much as to others – was that a single
opponent of union had been included, the notorious Jacobite,
George Lockhart of Carnwath.

It was soon the talk of the town that the omission of the Duke
of Hamilton explained the extraordinary absence of the Duke of
Argyll. Viewing Hamilton's motion to leave the selection of the
commissioners to the queen as an acceptance of the offer he had
made him, Argyll felt bound to honour his undertaking and had
included Hamilton in the list he had drawn up for presentation
to the queen. A number of members of the Squadrone Volante,
led by the Earl of Roxburgh, had gone to Queensberry and told
him that if Hamilton were included he would lose their support
in the negotiations. Hamilton, they said, would wreck them. However reasonable and yielding the English might turn out to be, the
duke would find something to insist on which would prove totally
unacceptable and would use it to rouse a popular revolt in
Scotland, which would cause the negotiations to be abandoned
and union ruined for all time. This had been the real reason, they
argued, for his acceptance of Argyll's offer and Argyll would be
mad to put his honour as a gentleman before the solid future of
his country.

Queensberry was a political realist. It was not he who had
given his word to Hamilton. Argyll had not consulted him. In any
case the offer had not been accepted at the time it was made.
Hamilton's strange move had come only after his discomfiture

over his Alien Act motion. Moreover, had he not been heard to say of his nomination proposal that, since it seemed no use to struggle further against the queen, he thought he might be allowed to pay her a compliment? It could be construed as a capitulation therefore, not a belated handclasp on a bargain. Even if it were a surrender, who could trust him to stay of that mind? Had he ever wholly committed himself to anything? Had he ever been known to answer a letter in his own hand? The Squadrone might be right or wrong in their reading of his intentions but they were clearly wise, Queensberry no doubt argued to Argyll, when they said he was the last man who should be numbered among the commissioners. The risk could not be taken. Honour or no honour, Hamilton was out. Upright Argyll angrily retorted that if there were no Duke of Hamilton on the commission there would be no Duke of Argyll, to which Queensberry coolly replied that for Scotland's sake he was content to be the only duke. So Argyll had sent in his resignation to the queen who appointed Queensberry in his place, and was taking his honour off to the Continent to fight for it there under Marlborough. Anti-unionists, of course, saw the whole episode as just another evidence of how Queensberry was rigging everything in preparation for his betrayal of Scotland.

Lockhart of Carnwath was more of a puzzle. Presumably he was there to represent the opposition to union under Hanover, a substitute for Hamilton, a single voice to be ignored, a single vote to be lost among the other thirty, but why bother to have him at all? He was the member of parliament for the county of Edinburgh (now Midlothian). He had inherited a considerable fortune made by his father and grandfather at the Scottish bar, was a nephew of the English Earl of Wharton, the Whig who had rescued Godolphin from the High Tory attempt to overthrow him after Blenheim, and in joining the Jacobites had gone to the extreme of opposition to the political tradition of his family for the past half-century. His father was Cromwell's Scottish legal adviser and represented Lanark in the Protector's United Parliament. At the Restoration he had apologised to Charles II on his knees for serving the usurper, but his repute with the king's opponents had been restored when in 1674 he became the cause of the first and only lawyers' strike in Scotland. He had advised a client to appeal to parliament against a judgment of the Court of Session. Government and judges condemned this as disrespectful of the royal justice and he was disbarred. Fifty of his fellow-advocates at once announced their withdrawal from practice until he should be restored. They were banished from Edinburgh and business in the courts was suspended for a year before a formula was proposed which allowed them to return. Lockhart senior was not himself immediately readmitted to the bar but his professional reputation mounted so high that within ten years it was impossible to avoid appointing him Lord President of the Court Session. He was shot dead in the High Street of Edinburgh in 1689 by a man who resented a judgment in favour of his wife in an alimony case.

The Lord President's brother, George Lockhart's uncle, had an equally distinguished career outside Scotland. Cromwell chose him to be Commonwealth ambassador in Paris and, when the general of the English and French forces co-operating against the Spaniards in Dunkirk during the war of 1655–58 fell ill, he took command and captured the town. Like his brother, he made his peace with Charles II who later sent him back to Paris to be his ambassador there. The brothers had never wholly abandoned the Presbyterian radical views which took them into Cromwell's service, so Jacobites were highly gratified when the heir to the Lockhart tradition and fortune forswore the former and began to devote the latter to furtherance of their cause. His relationship to a powerful English Whig family made him an even more notable defector. He had an impish sense of humour, loved putting the cat among the political pigeons, and was ready to be the cat himself when necessary. That propensity may account for his making so forthright a change of political allegiance when most of his contemporaries thought exchanging occasional discreet letters with somebody at St Germains enough to cover themselves. It no doubt amused him that his pronounced Jacobitism must have embarrassed a cousin who bore the name of Cromwell Lockhart. He made full use of all his parliamentary opportunities in a very efficient way and – more important for posterity – he was an acute observer and recorder of his fellows. He consulted with Atholl and the other Jacobites and they agreed he should accept the nomination as a commissioner in order to be their spy in the camp and alert them to possibilities of mischief.

In March the English commissioners were announced.

The thirty-one included the Archbishops of Canterbury and York, four dukes – Newcastle, Devonshire, Somerset and Bolton – two marquesses, Sir William Cowper (Lord Keeper of the Great Seal and Lord Chancellor), the two Chief Justices, the Speaker of the House of Commons, Godolphin, Somers, Halifax, Harley, Wharton, the Earl of Sunderland, Marlborough's son-in-law, and the three law officers of the crown. All were strong supporters of closer union with again a solitary exception – the Archbishop of York, High Churchman, High Tory, and outspoken hater of everything Scottish and Presbyterian.

The commissioners met on April 16 and nine weeks later pronounced themselves agreed on the contents of a Treaty of Union. The work had been done with a speed astonishing to both countries, because the leading commissioners were agreed before they sat down on the chief concessions to be made by both sides. The English had agreed among themselves that to get the Scots into as close a union as they needed for their military security they would give them all they wanted in the way of trade, and be generous about money to help lift Scotland out of poverty. The Scots leaders had agreed among themselves that to get the trade and what money they could they would sell their separate parliament. Both sides were agreed that if they were to get anywhere with the main issues they would have to forget about religion.

The great swap of the Scottish parliament for English trade was accomplished in nine days.

The commissioners had first to agree on procedure. They met in a building in Whitehall known as The Cockpit. No malice or cynicism seems to have influenced the choice of venue. The first day was given over to formal speeches by the two Lord Chancellors, Sir William Cowper for the English and the Earl of Seafield for the Scots, after which they adjourned for six days of private consultation. When they met again on April 22 Cowper moved that there should be no discussion in joint sessions. All matters should be debated by the two delegations in separate private meetings and they should meet together only to receive formal proposals and to hear formal replies, all of which should be submitted in writing. A small joint committee should agree minutes of the decisions. No decision should become binding until everything had been agreed, and everything should be kept top secret. The Scots had no objection to these business-like arrangements. Indeed, both sides so rigidly observed the ban on anything but written formal interchanges that they avoided even social meetings until the proceedings were over. 'No Scots or English', Lockhart of Carnwath recorded, 'met so much as to dine or drink a glass of wine.' Nobody was to be able to charge them with any salon or taproom conniving about so solemn an affair as a merger of nations. The necessary understandings had already been reached between Godolphin and Queensberry in the secrecy of the ministerial backstairs.

Among these was the sale of Scotland's parliament. It was considered desirable, however, that there should be some shadow-boxing, for the credit of the Scots commissioners with the public at home.

At the April 22 joint session Cowper formally moved that the two Kingdoms of England and Scotland be forever united into the Kingdom of Great Britain, that the United Kingdom of Great Britain be represented by one and the same parliament, and that the succession to the throne of Great Britain, in case of failure of heirs of Her Majesty's body, be according to the Act of Settlement of England (i.e. Hanover).

The Scots retired and came again two days later. Seafield announced that they agreed about the Hanover succession on condition that the subjects of both countries should enjoy equal rights and privileges, and that there should be free communication and intercourse of trade and navigation between them, and in the plantations (colonies), under such regulations as should be negotiated. They entered a formal objection to giving up their parliament.

The English retired and returned after a short interval. Nothing, Cowper said, would satisfy them but an entire incorporating union.

The Scots retired and came back again next day. All right, Seafield said, one parliament it is – if we are given the trade.

The English withdrew and returned after a brief pretence of discussion. They also had a public opinion to satisfy. Cowper announced that they accepted freedom of trade as a necessary consequence of an entire union.

The charade was over, the bargain had been openly struck, and a recess was agreed until April 29.

No bitter tears were shed in the Scottish delegation that night. The institution of parliament had not the place in the Scottish national heritage that it had with the English. Englishmen had been creating their parliament for nearly five hundred years, developing it to be the instrument through which order and justice could be maintained, and laws and taxes promulgated, with the consent of the elements in the nation which had established a claim to be consulted in the exercise of power. In 1706 the majority of the English population were still excluded from casting a vote for a member of parliament but the right had descended to the 'forty shilling freeholders' and the elections of members of the Commons were conducted with so much public canvassing, blatant bribery, and demonstration of party rivalry that everybody in the towns and villages was aware that an event of national and local importance was taking place and enjoyed some feeling of participation. Elections in Scotland were secretive affairs by comparison. The only electors in the country areas were the tenants-in-chief of the crown – largely descendants and successors of mediaeval feudal landlords – and relatives and friends whom they brought within the scope of the franchise by creating them feudal sub-tenants. Their total number in all the Scottish counties was under 2 700, an average of forty per elected member. It was possible, therefore, for the election of a member to be assured by pressure of one kind or another – kinship, friendship, patronage, bribery, intimidation – brought to bear on twenty to twenty-five voters, all of whom could be privately influenced over a bottle of wine in their homes or the backroom of an inn. Burgh members were elected by the select, self-perpetuating oligarchies of the burgh councils. Ordinary folk might know an election was going on, but nothing ever happened to give them any feeling that it had much to do with them. The Scottish single-chamber legislature mixed peers and commoners in a more egalitarian way than the English bi-cameral system, but the conjunction in the one chamber of rank and privilege with members selected in the private fashion described, conspired to remove Parliament still further away from all except the cronies of those with a hand in the electoral process. The commissioners who had agreed to an end to Scotland's parliament could assure themselves therefore that at most a few thousands of the population of a million would object to or mourn its passing for its own sake. 'The one Scottish institution,' say the historians Dicey and Rait, 'which never, except possibly for a moment before the passing of the Act of Union, kindled the enthusiasm of the Scottish people, has been the Parliament of Scotland.' The moment which Dicey and Rait refer to lasted for nine months and fills two chapters of this book. The commissioners were justified on all past showing, however, in believing that the mass of the nation would not care much, if at all, about the demise of their parliament.

The small number who might take a different view were some of the county and burgh electors and the members of parliament – although, unlike England, Scotland had no long history of parliamentary struggle. Before the short-lived revolt of the signatories to the National Covenant against Charles I the Scots parliament had met only to approve or disapprove, without debate, the measures placed before it by the Privy Council and prepared by the Committee of the Articles in accordance with the wishes of the king. Between the Restoration and the Glorious Revolution members who braved the royal displeasure could debate with the king's ministers, but legislation was still prepared by the Committee. Only in the past dozen years, since the Committee of the Articles had been abolished and members had been free to move and pass acts and resolutions of their own initiation, had there been any real enjoyment or satisfaction to be gained from having a seat in the parliament at Edinburgh. In these years many of the members had found an outlet in parliamentary speechmaking for emotions and energies which had formerly demanded the sword for adequate expression; they had given vent to impassioned patriotism, criticised and challenged authority, denounced tyranny and corruption, cried aloud national, group and personal grievances, ventilated reformist ideas, assaulted and insulted enemies – all with a reasonable expectation of nothing more serious than words in return. Many had developed a skill in oratory demonstrable by their fathers only in the law courts, the pulpit, and the General Assembly of the Kirk. Nobles and gentlemen no longer needed an education in law or divinity or a godly reputation to be entitled to parade their eloquence before their fellows. They might object, therefore, to exchanging the recently discovered prides and pleasures of the homely parliamentary life of Edinburgh for the unfamiliarities of Westminster. Patriots would no doubt argue that a separate parliament was essential to the preservation of Scottish nation-hood. Jacobites would strenuously resist any amalgamation of the parliaments whose purpose was to secure the Hanover succession in both countries.

There were no fervent patriots or parliamentarians among the Highland electorate. They voted in elections for or against the great Campbell, the Duke of Argyll. If against, they were automatically Jacobites and would therefore oppose a single parlia-ment; if Campbellites, they would support anything the duke supported, and he was for a single parliament. In the last twelve years parliament had begun to mean something to the lowland electorate. They were becoming aware that they had problems which would require action by parliament for their solution and that in electing a member they were choosing a spokesman. It was still all very new to them, however. Nothing had sunk into the marrow of their beings, as it had with the English, and their reactions to the proposal that the Scottish parliament should be abolished would probably follow those of their present parliamentary representatives.

The commissioners knew that, extreme patriotism and Jacobitism apart, the attitudes of present members were likely to be determined by personal situation, interest and ambition. If the entire Scottish parliament were offered seats at Westminster, the most influential factors would be age, health and wealth. London was at least three hundred miles farther away than Edinburgh from the home of every sitting member, a serious consideration for any who had reached middle age, loathed the thought of days of travel on horseback or in a lumbering coach or carriage, or could not afford the journey in addition to staying through a parliamentary session in the English capital, which would cost a great deal more than attending a parliament in Edinburgh. The young, the better off, and the very ambitious would discount the disadvantages, seeing Westminster as offering a more attractive stage for a parliamentary career than Edinburgh. (Most of the commissioners were themselves in one or more of these latter categories, or could expect to be compensated in some way for anything they might lose as a result of supporting the abolition of the Scottish parliament.) Old men, poor men, and bad travellers would join the extreme patriots and the Jacobites in opposing transition to Westminster. If the English insisted on

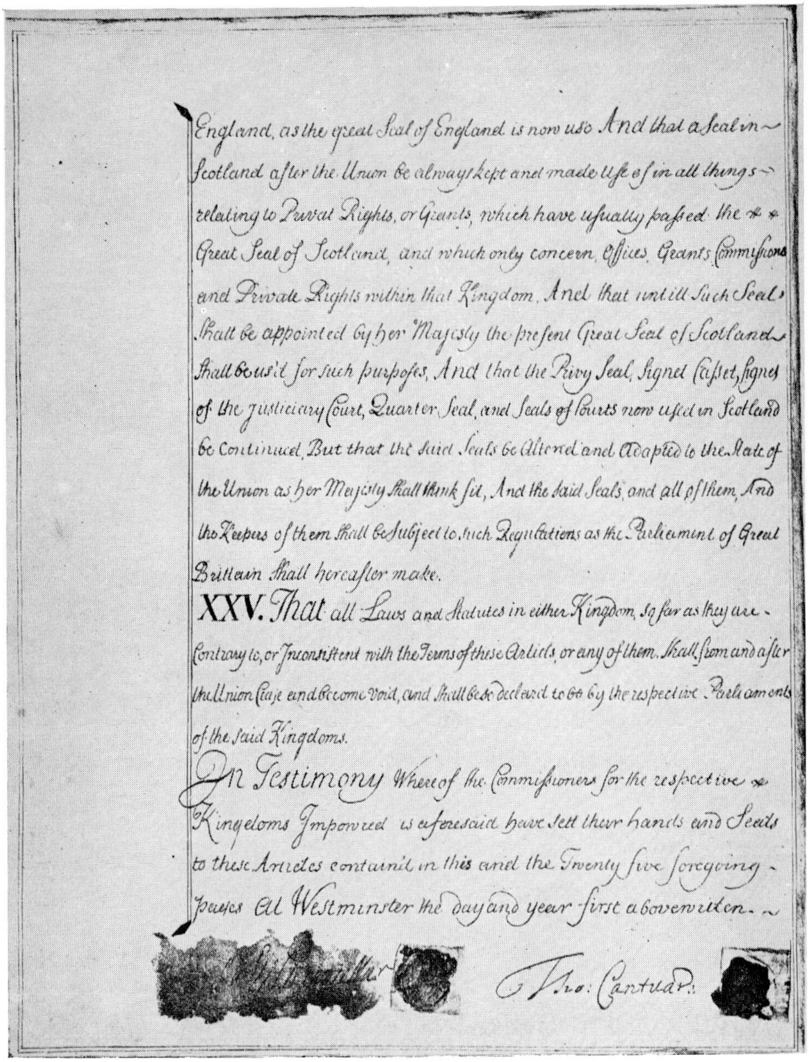

PLATE V

England, as the great Seal of England is now use And that a Seal in Scotland after the Union be always kept and made use of in all things relating to Privat Rights, or Grants, which have usually passed the Great Seal of Scotland, and which only concern Offices, Grants Commissions and Privat Rights within that Kingdom. And that untill such Seals shall be appointed by her Majesty the present Great Seal of Scotland shall be us'd for such purposes, And that the Privy Seal, Signet Casset, Signets of the Justiciary Court, Quarter Seal, and Seals of Courts now used in Scotland be continued, But that the said Seals be Altered and Adapted to the State of the Union as her Majesty shall think fit, And the said Seals and all of them, And the Keepers of them shall be subject to such Regulations as the Parliament of Great Brittain shall hereafter make.

XXV. That all Laws and Statutes in either Kingdom, so far as they are Contrary to, or Inconsistent with the Terms of these Articles, or any of them, shall from and after the Union Cease and become Void, and shall be so declared to be by the respective Parliaments of the said Kingdoms.

In Testimony Whereof the Commissioners for the respective Kingdoms Impowered is aforesaid have Sett their hands and Seals to these Articles contain'd in this and the Twenty five foregoing pages At Westminster the day and year first abovewritten.

The last page of the Treaty of Union as signed by 26 Scottish and 27 English Commissioners on July 22, 1706. The barely legible signature on the left is that of the Earl of Seafield, Scottish Lord Chancellor. The Archbishop of Canterbury signed first for England.

PLATE VI

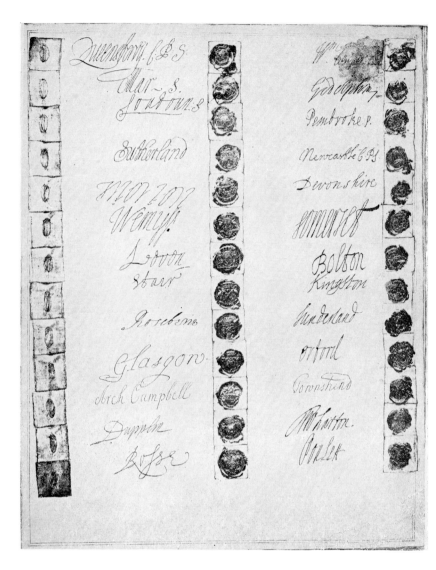

Another page of signatures to the Treaty of Union including, on the Scottish side: Queensberry, then Lord Privy Seal; Mar and Loudon, joint Secretaries of State; the Earl of Stair. Among the English signatories were Sir William Cowper, Lord Keeper of the Great Seal; the Earl of Godolphin, Lord High Treasurer; the Earl of Pembroke, Lord President of the Council; the Duke of Newcastle, Lord Privy Seal; Lord Wharton.

cutting down Scottish numbers, another group would be added: those who doubted their capacity to win election to a reduced representation.

Thus opposition within the nobility and the more articulate gentry might not be inconsiderable. The commissioners were not despondent about overcoming it, however. The patriots would be the most difficult for the commissioners were admittedly proposing to surrender with parliament any pretensions to an independent control of Scotland's earthly affairs. Even if the English agreed to combine the two parliaments as they stood, there were twice as many members in the two English houses as in the single Scottish chamber. But what other earthly affairs, they asked themselves that evening, compared in importance with the full bellies, warm backs, snug houses, and tidy balances in the new banks which the deal they were proposing gave Scotland's nobility and gentry an expectation of enjoying? This was the argument that had to be made to the patriotic, the old, the impecunious, the bad travellers, and the prospective election-losers. The choice was between parliament and trade, between the freedom to be poor and the right to be rich, between illusion and reality. It should not be impossible to make them see the alternatives, from whatever angle they might look. The single parliament was the one way, too, of ensuring peace between the two countries. Moreover, Protestantism was being secured, and Presbyterianism too for those to whom it was all-important, since it was understood on both sides of the negotiations that measures would be taken to protect the Kirk from any untoward consequences of the surrender of Scotland's parliamentary independence. This could well be a clinching argument with Presbyterians who welcomed the prospects of prosperity and peace but regretted the probable loss of their own participation in parliamentary debate, for Scotland would still have her General Assembly. The deprived godly could again find in it the sounding-board for their eloquence which had amply satisfied their fathers.

The question that had now to be tackled was finance – what and how Scotland would contribute to the expenses of the single kingdom. It took nearly a month to settle and a sub-committee of money and mathematics experts was needed to work out the details. The difficulty was that Scotland was poor, her taxes raised

E

considerably smaller sums per capita than England's, her expenditure was low and she had no national debt worth speaking about. England was rich, paid higher taxes, was spending a lot, and was accumulating a large national debt through her wars with the French. The Scots accepted that the equality with the English for which they had bargained must include proportionately equal taxation, and they were anticipating a time when equality of trading opportunity would put them in a position to bear it. That time was some way off, however, so while they accepted equality of taxation in principle, they argued for tax concessions over as long a period as possible. They were also unwilling to be taxed to meet expenditure on the debts incurred by England before the new union should come into force.

If the English had been difficult there was room here for interminable wrangling. They approached the problem, however, in a remarkably sympathetic and reasonable, even generous, way. Both sides knew that Scotland's great need was for cash in quantities adequate to prime the pump of prosperity and set it flowing, and this recognition prompted a method of overcoming the difficulties. If the Scots wanted a tax concession which the English could not grant, a calculation was made and a lump sum in lieu offered or asked for. If it were agreed, it was marked down under the heading of 'The Equivalent'. The same method was used with the debt obstacle, so that Scots taxes could be lumped with English after union and spent in meeting all national expenditure, including debt service and redemption, while the English would make a large immediate donation to the Equivalent.

In both countries revenue was raised mainly by customs and excise duties and a land tax. Equality of trade obliged the Scots to agree to the same customs duties on imports and exports as were imposed in England. The English agreed to time concessions in regard to the imposition in Scotland of excise duties on stamped paper, vellum, parchment, births, marriages and burials, windows and lights, coals and cinders. The Scots agreed to levy English rates of duty on beer, wines and spirits. Hackney carriages were passed over because there were so few in Scotland that it didn't seem to matter. The Scots suggested they should be exempted for a period from all new taxes imposed by the United Kingdom parliament. The English refused, but agreed that the Scots would not become subject to any new taxes imposed by the English parliament pending ratification of the treaty. There were protracted exchanges over malt and salt. The Scots objected to the tax on malt because it had been imposed in England specially to help pay for the war with France, in which the Scots claimed they had not been involved. The English eventually agreed that they need not pay it for the time being. Salt was important because it was the only means of keeping meat and fish from going bad and the Scots argued that a tax on it would be an intolerable burden on their many poor. Besides, they declared, the proceeds of England's salt tax were devoted entirely to reduction of the English national debt. The English offered exemption for seven years. The Scots replied that if they had to pay after seven years they would need another Equivalent to compensate them for contributing to English debt reduction. The English brought evidence to prove that the money was not all used for debt reduction but was spent also on encouraging trade and stood firm by their seven years' exemption. The trade evidence weakened the Scots and they finally gave way.

Both countries had a land tax. In England at four shillings on the pound of valued rent it raised £2 million. In Scotland parliament granted each year so many months 'cess', a sum fixed at £6 000, the number of months being decided by the amount it was thought necessary to raise. The Scots could not afford to change the method of the burden without risking the opposition of all landowners to union. The question was how a mere £6 000 a month could be related to an astronomical figure like £2 million. The mathematicians came up with an answer. They decided that England should be reckoned to be forty times richer than Scotland. One-fortieth of £2 million was £50 000. Eight months cess was £48 000, so round it down to that and say that an English tax of four shillings in the pound would be equal to eight months cess in Scotland. The formula seemed to the Scots to be politically practicable and so it was agreed.

The English were equally accommodating about the national debt part of the Equivalent. The mathematicians – among whom was William Paterson, founder of the Bank of England, happily recovered from the mental breakdown which followed the failure of his Darien scheme – again went to work to calculate how much of the revenues from Scottish customs and excise duties would go to service the English debt of more than £17 million, capitalised the sums at various rates, brought in the value of other concessions, and produced a total of £398 085 10s. The nice precision of the ten shillings silenced all cavilling. It was agreed that this sum, which would be paid over as soon as the treaty came into force, would be used to recompense Scots who sustained any losses through the adoption of a standardised coinage for the new United Kingdom, to reimburse investors in the Scottish Africa Company, to pay any debts the crown might owe to Scottish servants and subjects, and to subsidise wool manufacture, fishing and other industries in Scotland. Arrangments were made for further national debt Equivalents to be calculated when the increases in Scottish revenues expected from the improvement in trade should become apparent.

Both sides regarded the Equivalent as a sweetener for the pill of union which the Scots would hesitate to push from their lips, and the distribution of it had been devised to reduce opposition. Those who had lost money in the Darien venture would be most agreeably surprised. The crown creditors included some very influential nobles and gentlemen. The industrial subsidies would be welcome in many quarters. Because of the tax time-concessions, nobody need be very sorely hit – to begin with at any rate. The Scots commissioners thought they had come pretty well out of the financial negotiations.

The Scots had given away their parliament and by tacit agreement were keeping their General Assembly. They had now to decide what other institutions they wanted to preserve. Having got or bought what they most wanted, the English were easygoing about the rest, accepting what the Scots told them about their political necessities. The Scots proposed that while all laws regulating trade and taxation should be the same in Scotland as in England, in all other respects, civil and criminal, the law of Scotland and its legal machinery, institutions and practices should remain unaffected, except in so far as laws in the public domain might be amended at any future time by the new United Kingdom parliament. That body would not, however, be allowed to alter Scottish laws conferring rights on private individuals. The whole system of Scottish courts should be kept intact, including existing rights of landowners and royal burghs to execute justice within their own territories, and all heritable offices and privileges would be continued. English courts would have no power to review decisions and sentences of the Scottish courts or to interfere with their execution. The English appreciated the political expediency of these proposals. Not only would the votes of lawyers and land-owners determine the acceptibility of union in the Scottish parliament; the comfort of laws and courts to which they were accustomed was essential if union were to be tolerated by the Scottish people. They demurred at one thing only. The Scots courts could behave as quaintly as they liked on land but an English court must rule the sea. They insisted on a single Court of Admiralty, with appeals to the queen. The Scots agreed pro-vided they could keep a little court of their own for dealing solely with matters of landowners' private rights on the water.

There was a strange and important omission from the draft the Scots submitted forbidding English courts to interfere in Scotland. It mentioned the Courts of Chancery, Queen's Bench, Common Pleas and 'any other court in Westminster Hall' but made no reference to the House of Lords, the highest court of appeal in England, which did not sit in Westminster Hall. Scottish law was obscure as to whether there was a right of appeal to parliament against decisions of the Court of Session, and it may be that the Scots commissioners were unaware that they had not specifically excluded any appeal to a House of Lords of the new United Kingdom parliament. It may be that the English saw that the draft omitted the House of Lords and deliberately refrained from drawing attention to it. Perhaps both sides were aware of the omission and, as a Scottish historian has put it, 'indulged in one of the prudent ambiguities of cautious statesmen' by shutting an eye to it, and avoiding a clash which might have wrecked everything if it had to be settled at that moment as a matter of principle. The English would have found it difficult to agree to a lower status in the judicial system for the new United Kingdom House of Lords than that hitherto enjoyed by the English House. The Scots would have shrunk from telling their countrymen that the native legal system they were claiming to have preserved would be subject finally to an alien interpretation. There may have been an understanding among those commis-sioners on both sides who grasped the point that the best course was to say nothing until it should arise in practice, when it would be too late to unscramble the egg.

There were other nice examples of give and take. The Scots accepted English coinage and the English agreed that a mint should be maintained in Edinburgh. English law required that all trade be carried in home-built ships. Most Scottish ships had been built abroad because there was so little wood in Scotland, most of the forests having been burned over centuries and not replaced. The English agreed to accept Scottish foreign-built ships provided ship registration was transferred from Edinburgh to London. The Scots wanted their Scottish Africa Company to continue on the same footing as the English East India Company. The English insisted that the Scottish company be dissolved but agreed that the shareholders should be recompensed out of the money they were providing under the Equivalent. A new Great Seal would be adopted for the United Kingdom but the Scots could keep their own for domestic use. Separate Scottish records and registers would be maintained in Edinburgh.

The matter in which the English were least accommodating was Scottish representation in the United Kingdom parliament. It was not settled by the customary stately progress of the two bodies of commissioners from their separate chambers to stare in silence at each other while their spokesmen read out demands and responses, but was argued in joint session to prevent, it was said, the leaks that might occur if the stages of so delicate a negotiation had to be committed to paper. The English were determined that the numbers in their two chambers – five hundred and thirteen in the Commons and one hundred and ninety in the Lords – should remain intact. They were equally determined that there could be no simple incorporation of the numbers in the single-chamber Scots Parliament – over three hundred lords and commoners. The Scots, ready as before to be complaisant about their parliament, were willing to compromise. The difficulty was to find a formula for calculating a seemingly just proportion of Scots to English. They had gladly accepted to be forty times poorer than the English for the purposes of the land tax, but on this basis they would have had no more than a dozen representatives in the Commons and less than half a dozen in the Lords, and even the English agreed that this was less than their deserts. Population was looked at. There were no census figures in those days and estimates were only guesses. Some Scots claimed two million and granted the English six. But a one-third representation would have given the Scots one hundred and seventy-one in the Commons and sixty-three in the Lords, which the English considered far beyond their due. They picked a more reasonable figure out of the hat and suggested thirty-eight for the Commons. The Scots protested this was too low and forty-five was eventually agreed.

The number of peers was fixed at sixteen, to be elected by the existing Scottish peerage. A certain amount of haggling took place, not over the number of Scottish peers who could sit in the new House of Lords, but over the privileges Scottish peers in general should enjoy. English peers could not be prosecuted for debt while Scottish peers could. The Scottish peers among the commissioners thought the chance of dodging prosecution for debt was too good to be missed and said they would agree to be represented by sixteen of their number only if all Scottish peers became entitled to full English immunities and privileges. The English agreed to the immunities but reserved a privilege. They said only the sixteen elected Scottish peers should be entitled to sit in the House of Lords when the peers met to try one of themselves for treason or felony. The Scots were willing but wary. They attached a proviso that the sixteen should be able to take part in such trials if these should be held when parliament was not in session, thus insuring against a subterfuge by which the elected representatives of Scotland's ancient nobility might have been excluded from a trial, perhaps even of a Scottish peer. Nobody seems to have questioned the propriety of Scottish peers using union to immunise themselves against one of the old Scots laws they intended to take credit for preserving.

On June 28 a committee of four from each side was set up to put into the form of a treaty all the points that had been agreed, and May 1 of the following year was fixed as the target date for the new union to come into operation. Less than a month later, on July 22, 1706, the twenty-five articles of the Treaty of Union were signed by all but a handful of the sixty-two commissioners. Among those who did not attend the signing session were Lockhart of Carnwath and the Archbishop of York, the two who had been chosen to speak for the opponents of union. Anything Lockhart had said against it had gone unheeded and the Archbishop had saved his breath and his time. He ignored the whole business and did not attend a single session.

The following day the signed and sealed treaty was ceremoniously presented to Queen Anne in St James's Palace in the presence of the diplomatic corps and other notabilities. The commissioners came into the room like the animals into the ark, two by two, English and Scot side by side, and bowed. Lord Chancellor Seafield spoke for the Scots, Lord Keeper Cowper for the English. Anne clutched the document to her English heart and said the particulars of it seemed so reasonable 'that I hope they will meet with approbation in the Parliaments of both kingdoms. I wish therefore that my servants of Scotland may lose no time in going down to propose it to my subjects of that kingdom and I shall always look upon it as a particular happiness if this union, which will be so great a security and advantage to both kingdoms, can be accomplished in my reign.'

'And thus', says Daniel Defoe, 'this mighty affair was brought to a conclusion.'

Defoe was anticipating, of course. A treaty had been signed on behalf of the two countries. As Anne had said, it had now to win the approval of the parliaments of both countries. The English political leaders were confident of the outcome at Westminster if they could present it while they held their majority. The Scots could not be so certain. They had got so far only by the skin of their teeth, and though the treaty had been skilfully constructed to wear down the parliamentary opposition they knew it might take time. There was much the rabble-rousers could be using in the meanwhile to inflame the country. Hence Anne's request to them to hurry and the decision to put the treaty first to the parliament of Scotland. It would not help its fate with the Scots if they were asked to swallow something the English had already digested.

As they stood before the queen, however, the commissioners felt themselves entitled to congratulations from the ambassadors of the countries which regarded it as a good thing for Europe and the world that England and Scotland should be coming closer together. They had met to strike a bargain and they had done it.

Anne had summed it up succinctly when she spoke of security and advantage. The English had bought security and the Scots had bought advantage. The approach on both sides had been intensely practical. There had been no social philosophers among them elaborating theories of how two peoples whom geography had thrown together on the same island, and whom history had conditioned to hatred on the one side and contempt on the other, could best learn to live in amity under one government. Nobody had tried to look beyond his nose; only immediate needs had been considered. Nevertheless, the interplay of strategic, economic, political, class and personal interests had resulted in a scheme of union whose broad features could scarcely have been bettered by any philosopher then or since.

The Scots have been faulted by their countrymen in more recent times for giving up their parliament. They underrated the importance of that institution and could be said to have been short-sighted in agreeing to the total transfer of policy-making and administration to London. It was, however, the price they knew they must pay to get Scotland on the road to economic betterment, and they genuinely believed that they and their countrymen had more to gain from warehouses than parliament houses. The English politicians are not to be blamed for insisting on the transfer of everything to London. At the time the chief functions of government were to defend the country, maintain law and order, and see that the citizens were enabled to seek prosperity and enjoy it. It seemed obvious to them that for these purposes one government was to be preferred to two within an island, and at that time there were no strong arguments to set against their view. The great swap appeared sound and statesmanlike to the men who made it.

Both sides had shown wisdom rather beyond their time in agreeing that the union they were negotiating did not demand a single national church or a single system of laws and courts. Political expedience rather than reasoned principle made the two separations so readily acceptable to the English, since a peaceful union would have been impossible without them. The agreement to unite with these diversities permitted the Scots to maintain and develop some of their differences from the English while at the same time becoming more like them and more liked by them. It has kept the Scots a nation within a nation without the bitterness and strife which has dogged other such attempted unions. It was the first big step of the English on the path of the toleration which became their national characteristic and pride. They deserve some credit for it, however motivated.

None of the English commissioners had anything to gain personally from uniting England with Scotland, except in so far as their political interests and ambitions were being served by securing the Hanover succession and the safety of the country. The Scots were more open to charges of selling their country for personal advantage and these were soon being made. They were even to be accused of bribery and corruption. Certainly there were some among them who were influenced by the prospects of improving their own fortunes in the increase of national prosperity which they believed union would bring to Scotland. Noble members of the commission were no doubt attracted by the more dazzling social and political opportunities promised by mixing on an equal footing with their fellows across the border, particularly if their rents and investment possibilities grew as satisfactorily in consequence of union as they hoped they would. All who had signed the treaty had done so in the conviction that they and their families and friends had little to lose and probably something to gain from its implementation. They were not all moved solely by self-interest, however. Most of them had come to believe that what could be good for them would in the long run be good for Scotland, a belief which men of their type and position were prone to hold; but they had not all ceased to be patriots and in reaching this belief there had been genuine heart-searching. If it is accepted that a time had come when it was in the general interest to end the circumstances which were keeping the two peoples of the island apart, the Scots commissioners must be credited with having done as good a job for their country as the ideas and conditions of the time permitted. It should also be remembered that they were working under pressure. As they saw it, union had to be effected then and there if the Scots were to be kept from attacking the English in anger and the English from invading Scotland in fear of an enemy who was threatening to use the separation of the two countries to play havoc with both. Part of the credit for the Treaty of Union – and perhaps of the blame too, if blame there can reasonably be – should go to Louis XIV, under whose menacing shadow it was made.

8 Twenty-six against a Nation

In spite of Queen Anne's exhortation to them to lose no time in proposing the treaty to her Scottish subjects, her ministers delayed summoning parliament until October.

There was method in their dilatoriness. Twenty-six of the thirty-one Scottish commissioners had signed the treaty in London. When they returned to Edinburgh at the end of June these twenty-six were probably the only Scots who were ready to say they had done the right thing. Nobody had expected their mission to be successful, at least not within the brief time they had taken to accomplish it. When news got round that a new union had been signed and sealed and was to be presented to parliament for ratification, it was heard everywhere with astonishment and panic. Nine out of ten Scots leaped at once to the conclusion that they were the victims of a sell-out. They had never hoped that any good for them could come out of England. Since the bargain had been made so swiftly it could mean one thing only: Scotland's representatives had tamely submitted to everything the English had demanded and had sold them to be England's slaves. 'Treaters, traitors,' was the cry that rang immediately through the tall Edinburgh tenements, and rapidly echoed from every hilltop between Wick and Stranraer.

The twenty-six decided to postpone taking on the nation until October because they wanted winter on their side. However much the anger of the people might froth and bubble, they banked on its not boiling over into insurrection until the parliamentary debate had begun and decision seemed imminent. If the crucial period could be deferred until November or December, when the autumn rains turned roads and tracks into mud in which marching men sank up to the knees, and the snow on the hills was a shivery reminders of the dark and icy rigours of improvised campaigning in January and February, they would be safe from a national uprising until spring when, with a bit of luck, the formal debate might be over and the fever might have subsided. The canny Scots were never quite so angry in the winter as they could be in the summer. However, the Scottish parliament had never before met in the winter and its opening could not be deferred beyond October if the members were to reach Edinburgh while the roads were still passable. The May deadline was also to be remembered. No one could forecast how long the debate might last with twenty-five articles to be separately fought over, line by line and word by word.

There were risks in procrastination. The opponents of union would have the good months of July, August and September to roam the country with their tales of the horrors the treaty threatened, and the twenty-six were well aware that there was little they could do to counter such propaganda, so far as the common people were concerned. Most would remain stubbornly and bitterly opposed no matter what was said to them in favour and would believe the worst they were told, however fantastic. There was nothing to be done, except wait for winter to repress them. The same three good months, on the other hand, could be used by the twenty-six to inform members of parliament and influential electors in the counties and burghs, by letter and visit, of the arguments for the treaty, and so build up a solid body of support in the House to put it through regardless of the voteless common folk. A job of selective education had to be done and three months was not too long for it to be successful. Winter would not protect them from the fury of the mob in Edinburgh and its vicinity, but there were three thousand troops whose muskets and bayonets could be called upon, and while these were insufficient to keep the nation down in the summer months, they should be enough to hold the capital in check if winter were isolating it from the rest of the country.

In spite of their poverty the Scots were the most literate people in Europe, thanks to the parish schools founded by John Knox. Before July was out a stream of anti-union pamphlets was coming off the presses and being distributed to the towns and villages. Copies were handed from house to house, cottage to cottage, read aloud to family gatherings. The pamphleteers had four lines of attack: loss of independence and the consequent disappearance of the Scottish nation from the peoples of the world; the feeble representation of Scotland in the proposed United Kingdom parliament and the consequent danger to the Kirk; the burden of the English taxation which Scots would have to pay; the deception that was being worked on Scotland in the offer of free trade.

The first was held to be self-evident from the acquiescence in a foreign succession to the crown, the abolition of the national parliament, and the admission of English tax-gatherers and excisemen. The second was rammed home by a comparison. The Scottish nation would be represented in the United Kingdom House of Commons by forty-five members. The remote county of Cornwall, a rocky end of England poking out into the Atlantic, sent to Westminster no fewer than forty-four members. Scotland was being reduced to the level of a single English county and that neither the largest nor the richest. The insult was intolerable to a proud people whose history was as long as that of the English, whom even the Romans had never conquered and whose kings had sat on England's throne. What could forty-five Scots do against five hundred English when the weapons were voices and votes and no longer swords and spears? Scotland was to have sixteen peers in the Lords, where they would be outnumbered by the English bishops, the arch-enemies of the Kirk and representatives of all that was spiritually anathema to Presbyterian Scots. The first time that the union Parliament met the bishops would introduce a bill for the abolition of the Kirk and pass it against the Scots by their episcopal votes alone, without needing any help from the hundred other peers who would applaud enthusiastically. As for taxation, the English paid duties on salt and malt. If Scots had to pay on these, they would be unable to afford either food to eat or beer to drink. The swap of independence for freedom of trade was a blatant cheat. All English trade was conducted by monopoly companies which would continue to have complete control of it. Scotland was giving away everything for nothing and would not benefit by a groat. The English were a faithless, wicked and abominable nation who were seeking to obtain by trickery the conquest of Scotland which they had never accomplished by force of arms. The twenty-six signing 'treaters' were indeed twenty-six traitors whom it was the duty of all true Scots to repudiate and if necessary exterminate. The treaty was a judgment of God on Scotland for the sins of forgetfulness of her national heritage and indifference to the insults and injuries heaped upon her during the last hundred years. The only way to escape the judgment was to tear the treaty up and the treaters limb from limb and either remain for evermore proudly independent or make a commercial alliance with the French.

For three months the treater-traitors reasoned with everybody they thought it worth while to reach. They declared independence to have become a dangerous illusion. The events of the past century had demonstrated that it was impossible, within an island of the size of Britain, so inevitably involved in the politics of Europe, to have two governments attempting to follow conflicting policies under one crown. Two crowns were nowadays even more impossible. Bitter as it might be to Scots, the hard fact had to be faced that the peace of both countries in the island demanded that they should be under one crown and one government. If Scots did not accept the necessity voluntarily, it would not be long before England would be compelled to impose it on them by force. Scotland could not resist without foreign aid and France was the only quarter from which aid could come. England now had command of the seas and was likely to maintain it indefinitely, so French reinforcements would probably not be forthcoming. Marlborough's victories at Blenheim and Ramillies had shown England's military and political strength and she could probably take an invasion of Scotland in her stride with hardly any interruption of her ability, helped by her allies, to contain the French power. There was small hope, therefore, of preventing the English from imposing union by force. Supposing, however, Louis succeeded by some miracle in sending troops to aid the Scots, independence would not be preserved for long unless England were defeated, not only inside Scotland but also in her whole war with the French. In that case Louis would be master, not only of Europe, but also of Scotland, and would not be able to relax his hold on her since she would be strategically necessary to him for keeping England weak and subservient. He would not feel safe in these circumstances with a Presbyterian Scotland. To satisfy him she would have to be under Catholic domination. The military alternatives therefore were conquest by England or enslavement by Catholics. Surely it made sense to effect a peaceful union with England while opportunity offered.

Besides, what kind of independence was Scotland losing? She could not afford a navy to protect her shores or her merchant ships, even if she could afford any of the latter. Her army of three thousand men, which she barely had money to maintain, was insufficient to protect the lowlands from the Highland clans. She could not afford a permanent representative in any country in the world. Her commerce, industry and agriculture lagged a century behind those of the English and the Dutch. She was losing nothing by union except the freedom to stay poor. She would keep her religion and her laws, all existing rights and privileges. She was being given time to adjust herself to any new taxation and means to find the wherewithal to meet it, as well as cash to start her off on a new life. The doors of the world were being opened to her. Rejection of the treaty would not preserve her independence and held out no promise of anything but hazard to life and property and increasing misery and poverty. Acceptance offered a near certainty of some improvement in the personal circumstances of all those to whom the twenty-six addressed themselves.

By the end of September the twenty-six were able to see how the country was dividing.

Edinburgh was against them, masses and tradespeople. A hundred years ago they had lost the royal court to London. Now they were to lose the parliament. Nothing would be left to sustain the status of a capital but the law courts and the Kirk's General Assembly. The nobility and gentry would desert them. Litigants and divines were not spenders and the mob would have nobody to stare at or harry.

The surrounding counties, or at least those people in them who mattered, were for union. Their part of the country was ripest for the economic progress the unionists were promising and would suffer most if the English invaded. Most of the east coast up to Aberdeen was pro-union too, and the majority of Glasgow merchants had been won over. Their eyes were on the tobacco and sugar plantations of the West Indies and America.

The people north of Aberdeen and in the central and western Highlands were still firmly anti-union. There was nothing in the treaty to appeal much to Jacobites and Catholics. Lanarkshire, Stirlingshire, Renfrewshire, Ayrshire and the three counties on the Solway Firth were the problem area. Strongholds of the fiercely Presbyterian covenanting tradition of the seventies and eighties of the previous century, they were the most affected by the propaganda of the pamphleteers about the menace of the bishops in the House of Lords, and the least willing to forget the memories of harsh rule from London.

Such was the broad picture, but even in the most favourable areas there was no solidity for union. Lairds and tenants were opposed to one another, fathers and sons, brother and brother.

Only votes in parliament mattered to the twenty-six at the moment, however, and while there was yet no certain majority to count on for three months' hard work the outlook was not unhopeful. Whether or not a majority would be obtainable would be determined by the attitude of the Kirk.

At the end of September an official pronouncement from the Kirk was still being awaited. The governing body, the General Assembly of ministers and laity, was not due to meet until the following April. Between assemblies decisions on matters of urgency could be made by a committee of leading ministers which was then in anxious session in Edinburgh. The Kirk still had its fire-eaters but they were by no means as numerous as they had been in earlier generations. The ministry as a whole no longer aspired to tell governments what they must do to fulfil the will of God in Scotland. They or their predecessors had taken a severe battering in the previous half-century, and some of the sophistication which distinguished the contemporary gentry and nobility from their counterparts in the times of John Knox and James VI had been rubbing off on them. They were less sure that there had been a parallel in Israel for everything in the modern world and that the Hebrew prophets were infallible guides to choosing between Stuart and Hanover or poverty and economic development. They accepted that there were functions of secular government and administration which might have to be conducted beyond and around the machinery of the Kirk, and their chief concern now was to keep it and the faith free of statutory encroachment. The twenty-six had not neglected the important men of the Kirk, and while the great national controversy could not be kept out of the pulpit and the preachers were not concealing the fears of union which they shared with their congregations, their sermons had for the most part taken the form of questioning and lamentation rather than outright denunciation and incitement to rejection. They were exercising restraint, not because they doubted that union meant loss and suffering for the country's poor, but because the word had gone round that it could conceivably be the least of the evils threatening the Kirk. A seed had been sown by the pro-union politicians in the minds of the more tractable members of the Edinburgh committee, and they were wrestling with themselves and their fellows in debate and prayer.

The hope of the twenty-six that the debate would not be unduly prolonged rested on the chairman of the committee, William Carstares, Principal of Edinburgh University and current Moderator of the Assembly. Among Carstares' papers is an unsigned letter containing the sentence: 'The union could never have had the consent of the Scottish Parliament if you had not acted the worthy part you did.' Who paid this tribute to Carstares is not known but its assessment of the value to the union protagonists of having a man of his calibre, experience and outlook in the office of Moderator at this juncture is not exaggerated. He was the eldest of the nine children of a Cathcart covenanting minister who had been forced into hiding from Lauderdale's dragoons. The son had been sent to Holland to complete his education for the ministry and, on returning, he was incarcerated in Edinburgh Castle for five years for distributing anti-Lauderdale literature. He went back to Holland when released, became involved in the plots against James II, was captured on a secret mission in Kent, released after torture, and allowed again to go to Holland. He attracted the attention of William of Orange who made him his chaplain. He conducted the thanksgiving service after William's landing at Torbay and from this time he was the king's constant companion and adviser on Scottish and religious matters, William regarding him a 'a truly honest man', no small recommendation in those double-dealing days. His advice was fearless and disinterested and frequently taken. High Church Anne had no use for a Presbyterian divine in her entourage, so Edinburgh Town Council made him principal of the university, and his handling of students, professors and councillors in the previous two years had won unqualified admiration. the ministers who had elected him Moderator were all well aware how much the unusual peace of mind the Kirk had enjoyed under William

had been due to Carstares. Most members of the committee were
disposed to believe that any advice he gave about union would
be genuinely in the interests of the Kirk and the country as he saw
them, and the next best thing to a direct divine answer to their
prayers. Carstares had a deep respect for his late royal master's
political sagacity. William had always thought a closer union of
England and Scotland should come about as soon as possible for
the good of both countries as well as his own goal of European
stability. Carstares had no doubt therefore that he should lead the
Kirk towards acceptance of the opportunity offered by the Treaty.
He was confident that the growth of the movement towards
religious toleration in England, and the strength of its representation in the Westminster parliament, would safeguard the Kirk
against episcopal invasion of its status and privileges. But he
could not expect his colleagues to share his faith in the future.
Safeguards had to be made immediate and visible for them. He
appreciated that such safeguards could not be woven into the
fabric of the treaty and that his powers of persuasion must be
directed to convincing his fellow-ministers that they could safely
be sought elsewhere. He was a patient man and skilled in the
intricacies of Presbyterian argument. He assured the twenty-six he
would take no longer than was necessary to ensure that when the
Kirk committee spoke it would be with a pro-union voice.

Hostile Edinburgh was in a ferment when parliament met on
October 3. The mob cheered the Dukes of Hamilton and Atholl,
Lockhart of Carnwath, and other known opponents of union,
cursed Queensberry, Seafield, the Earls of Stair and Mar, and the
other commissioners, and threatened their lives if they did not
drop the treaty. The Duke of Argyll had taken leave from the
army to lend his weight in the debating and voting, and received
his share of the execration. Treaty supporters dared not venture
out of doors without bodyguards of armed servants. The canyons
of tall houses reverberated with the shouts of 'No union' and
'Treaters, traitors'. In the House the treaty was read through
and ordered to be printed. There were various items of routine
business to be transacted and two weeks passed before it was discussed again. In the interval members were bombarded with
letters from their constituencies imploring them to vote against
it, and the crowds demonstrated so continually outside the

residences of members whom they suspected of being for it that those who could not muster sufficient protection found it safer to go into disguise and hiding. Similar tumults occurred in other towns where the citizens had not been given satisfactory assurances by the magistrates that they were doing everything in their power to hold the burgh member to rejection. A movement spread rapidly through the country for monster petitions to be signed in counties, burghs and parishes, and presented to parliament. The committee of ministers of the Kirk discussed motions that they should ask parliament not to decide the issue of union until the General Assembly could meet in April, and that the queen should be petitioned to convene an earlier assembly. Both were turned down as being specious delaying devices which the government was certain to refuse and all the hamstrung committee could nerve itself to do was to request the congregation in every parish to pray fervently that God should show parliament the best thing to do for the Kirk.

The opposition's first attack when the House returned to the treaty was on the constitutional right of parliament to decide so important a question as its own extinction and the loss of the country's independence without a specific mandate from the electorate. There had been no election for some years and the present membership had no authority to determine the whole future of the country. An adjournment was moved to allow the members to consult with their constituents and receive their instructions. The government argued that the queen had summoned this session specially to conclude a treaty of union and that there were precedents for deciding constitutional issues without consulting the electors. Nobody had suggested such consultation when parliament gave the crown to William and Mary or when the present membership had passed the Act of Security. Opposition supporters may have resented the suggestion that they were not free to cast their votes as they wished, or the waverers may have been reluctant to have their discretion circumscribed; anyhow, the government got a large majority. The issue was far from being settled but the House had at least decided to keep it in its own hands.

Opposition leaders retaliated by proposing a day of national fasting and supplication. They had been frustrated in an appeal to the electorate. The government could not so easily squash a

national appeal to Almighty God, and if anger could be
sharpened by hunger and puffed up by large doses of Presbyterian prayer the consequences might be explosive. The government staved the move off for the moment by agreeing that it
should be referred to the committee of the Kirk.

Three days later the House started a formal reading of each
of the treaty's twenty-five articles, the first of which united the
two kingdoms forever into one under the name of Great Britain.
The opposition moved a delay of eight days to give time for
members to search their consciences before taking the fatal step.
The government could not afford to let momentum slacken but
they were anxious not to rush their fences and invite a fall. They
proposed instead that no vote should be taken on any article until
they had all been read and debated. This was a neat manoeuvre,
because it appeared to give plenty of time for conscience-probing
while allowing business to proceed. A canter round the whole
course without jumps being attempted seemed the very thing to
calm the terrors of the nervous and on the second round they
might take the hazards at a gallop.

At this juncture the Kirk committee delivered the recommendation the government had been waiting and angling for. A
majority of the ministers agreed that, since God in His infinite
and inscrutable wisdom seemed to have given Scotland no option
but to unite or be united with England or France, an Episcopalian devil was preferable to a Catholic one. They recommended
that steps be taken to incorporate in the treaty a provision to
secure the Kirk for all time from any amendment by crown or
parliament of its doctrine, discipline, worship or government.
If that were done, the Kirk was willing to support union with
England. The offer was reported to the House and the government gladly undertook to take it up and deal with it before the
business of the treaty was concluded.

The Kirk committee and the government now felt they could
more safely allow the people to request God's guidance, so on
October 21 national fasting and prayer was inaugurated at a
service in St Giles Cathedral attended by Queensberry as Lord
High Commissioner, Seafield as Lord Chancellor, other members
of the government, the other treaty negotiators, and most of the
Presbyterian members of parliament. Services were held in other
towns and all passed off without untoward incident. Taking their

cue from the committee, the ministers restricted their sermons
and prayers to a modest hope that Providence would be with
parliament in its deliberations and lead it along the way the Kirk
had indicated it was ready to go. The twenty-six said their own
quiet prayers of thankfulness. They would have to keep their
fingers crossed but there might now be enough votes to see them
through.

Congregations at the services were too stunned and be-
wildered by the desertion of their spiritual advisers to protest.
Recovery was swift in Edinburgh. Two days after the St Giles
service real violence broke out. While the House had been re-
connoitring the articles agitators had been busy outside, claiming
that the government was marking time on the voting solely because
it was afraid. Union supporters would scatter in terror if the mob
rose. Parliament would dissolve. The troops were anti-union and
would refuse to shoot. The time had come to strike. The royal
crown, sword and sceptre, the ancient 'Honours' of Scotland and
symbols of its independence, were about to be removed from
Holyrood to London. The mob should seize the Honours, carry
them to the Castle, and defy the government of traitors.

The Duke of Hamilton had developed a lameness and was
being taken to and from parliament in a chair. When the House
rose on October 23 the mob carried him down the street in a
wild ecstasy of adulation, and hurled filth at Queensberry
over the heads of his escort. They were battering down the door
of the house of Patrick Johnson, a treaty commissioner and
lately Lord Provost of the city, when the town guard arrived and
valiantly arrested six of the ringleaders. Blood was up, however,
and soon bands were roving through the town smashing the
windows of houses in which members of parliament were known
to be residing, extinguishing lights, and stoning respectable
citizens who dared to look out at them. By nine o'clock that
evening they had driven the local forces of law and order off the
streets and were besieging them in the gate-houses into which they
had retreated. Queensberry sent a party of footguards from
Holyrood round the outside of the town wall to the Netherbow
Port to hold it and prevent the rioters from blocking all movement in or out of the city they now dominated. The military were
banned from entering the city precincts without the permission

of the Lord Provost, and Queensberry sent to ask it. A thousand
fishermen and seamen were reported to be mustering to march
from Leith to join the Edinburgh rabble who were flourishing
arms and beating drums. Unless the government quickly showed
its ability to restore order the situation could go beyond retrieval.
The sympathies of the magistrates were with the mob but they
shrank from bloody revolution. The Lord Provost at last gave
the word and after midnight a battalion from the Castle, led by
the Duke of Argyll, marched through the town and drove the
rioters, who lacked effective leadership, back into their closes,
wynds and vennels. Next day three foot regiments took up quarters
around the city. Horse guards escorted Queensberry and other
members of the government, and the Castle garrison was
strengthened. The Privy Council issued a proclamation forbidding meeting and marching in the streets and required the
deacons of the trade guilds to obtain from their members
securities for the good behaviour of their servants and apprentices.
Officers and men of the army were indemnified against charges
arising out of any wounding and killing of citizens.

Edinburgh was placed under martial law.

The opposition could not accept this suppression of popular
feeling without protest. Hamilton and Atholl declaimed angrily
in the House that free speech was being denied and the country
dragooned into union. The real purpose of the military dis-
positions was not to control a mob but to overawe parliament: it
was the start of a reign of terror aimed at enslaving the nation.
Military rule in the capital was incompatible with the freedom of
parliament, the safety of whose members was the responsibility of
the magistrates of Edinburgh. The rhetoric fell flat, however,
when the unhappy magistrates confessed their inability to safeguard their own lives and property without military help, far
less the lives of men from other parts who had lost favour with the
populace. Members were by now so conscious of the risks they ran
that they not only approved maintenance of a military presence
in Edinburgh but repealed the authority they had given some time
earlier for gentlemen to raise their own militia for defence against
the English. They felt it had become a dangerous power to leave
active in the country in their absence.

The canter round the treaty course lasted a fortnight. The

opposition tactic was to hold the strength of their oratorical fire
for the next stage, in which the votes would be taken, and prepare
the ground for amendments to the treaty which would ensure its
rejection by the English parliament if it were not rejected outright
by the Scots.

They argued for a federal rather than an incorporating union,
if union there must be, with Scotland keeping her own parliament.
They demanded that if there had to be one parliament it should
be composed of the entire membership of both present parliaments,
giving Scotland some three hundred members against England's
seven hundred. They demonstrated how inhuman and im-
practicable it would be to ask Scots to pay the monstrous English
taxes. They compared the £398 085 10s. Equivalent which the
Scots were being offered with the mountainous £17 million debt
they would be shouldering and lamented over the bond slavery
into which the commissioners were proposing to sell their country's
children. Patiently the government and the commissioners
addressed themselves to the uncommitted members, explaining
why it had to be the treaty and nothing but the treaty. They
agreed to set up a committee to examine customs and excise
duties and the amount of the Equivalent, with the expert help of
the Professors of Mathematics of Aberdeen and Edinburgh
Universities.

When the last article had been read on October 30 the twenty-
six felt reasonably sure the main issue would be decided in their
favour. Of course on the morrow the chief opposition spokesmen
would open the floodgates of patriotic emotion, and there was no
saying how many of the floating votes that the government had
been guiding so delicately to their side might be tossed back into
midstream and land on the wrong bank when the House was
divided on the crucial first article. The current from the Kirk was
running steadily in the right direction, however, and the turbu-
lence from Edinburgh had been dammed. Hamilton and Atholl
had attacked the treaty relentlessly, but Hamilton had been having
some curious conversations with members of the government and
hopes were entertained that when it came to the vote he might
turn another somersault. He was still the idol of the subdued
crowds in Edinburgh High Street, and the masses of the country
were looking to him to bring off the miracle the ministers of the

Kirk were suggesting should no longer be expected of God. But Atholl had been seen to glance strangely at him and they were not as close as the occasion seemed to demand. Atholl consistently damned everything. If one listened carefully to Hamilton's tirades it was possible to fancy that he was lessening his resistance again on some things – Hanover for instance. He could be preparing for a split with Atholl on the morrow.

How big a rising throughout the country might be sparked off by a vote for the treaty in parliament was still an open question. The tinder was there in plenty and firebrands were not lacking. Colonel Erskine, the Provost of Stirling, for example, had paraded the local militia, and with his drawn sword in one hand and a pen in the other had collected signatures for one of the petitions against union which were on their way to Edinburgh and would start being formally presented to the House tomorrow. Other gentlemen in the midland and border counties were rattling arms and the peasantry were eager to follow them. Highland chiefs had their clansmen on the alert for a fiery cross, which they daily expected. Queensberry's agents estimated that fifteen to twenty thousand men were ready to march if they were given the word. The question which none of the government agents was able to answer was who was likely to give the word. It would not be Hamilton (his mother had, significantly, threatened to evict any Hamilton tenants who took up arms) and there was no information that Atholl or any other Jacobite was busying himself with anything other than his parliamentary activities. No foreign agent was known to be unusually active. Although probably two out of every three men of consequence in the country were against union, it could be that none of them was prepared personally to do more to prevent it than sign a piece of paper and wait for someone else to make a move. It remained to be seen how many had even signed the petitions. Examination of the one awaiting presentation from the county of Midlothian showed that, of some two hundred men of some substance in the county, not more than a dozen had put their names to it.

There were nearly a million common folk and there was no saying what they might do, spontaneously, if the House voted against their wishes. It was only the end of October and winter had not set in. It would take at least a thousand troops to keep the Edinburgh mob under control. The remaining two thousand would quickly be swept away if an outbreak of fighting in the lowlands brought down the wild Highlanders.

The government took no chances. They asked London to have English reinforcements standing by across the border and in Ireland.

9 The End of a Kingdom

It took four bleak November days to get down to the crucial voting on the first three articles – four days of obstruction, presentation of petitions from the country, and impassioned speeches.

The opposition moved once more for time to consult the electorate, were defeated, and tried hard to argue that the English parliament should vote first. Why should the English not say how they liked the water before Scotland took the plunge? England had nothing to lose, Scotland everything. Let her declare her mind. The government replied that it was now or never. The House, having reached the brink, voted to stay there.

It was also now or never for the petition-organisers. Just short of a hundred, all against the treaty, were presented from counties, burghs and parishes. 'We therefore supplicate and do assuredly expect,' ended the petition from the Convention of Royal Burghs, 'that ye will not conclude such an incorporate union as is contained in the articles proposed but that ye will support and maintain the true reformed Protestant religion and church government as by law established, the sovereignty and independency of this Crown and Kingdom, and the rights and privileges of Parliament, and do further pray that effectual means may be used for securing this nation against all the attempts and encroachments by any persons whatsoever upon the sovereignty, laws, liberties, trade, and quiet of the same. And we promise to maintain with all our lives and fortunes all these valuable things.'

The government had no qualms about leaving the petitions on the table. There were thirty-four counties, sixty-six burghs and nine hundred and thirty-eight parishes in the country. Fourteen counties petitioned and only sixty parishes. Of sixty-six burghs, twenty-four had voted for the draft of the Convention's petition, twenty against, and the rest had not bothered to be represented.

The petitioners all put the Kirk first and it had been agreed to take care of that. Petitions heaviest with signatures came from areas that had little prospect of greater prosperity, with or without union. Burghs with economic possibilities were significantly absent from the petition list.

Two concessions were made to still hesitant parliamentarians: no vote on any article would irrevocably commit anybody until all the articles had been voted on; and, to soothe those who were anxious about the Kirk, a measure to safeguard it would be introduced if the first article uniting the kingdoms were carried, and would be disposed of before votes were cast on the next article. The opposition clamoured that the vote on the Kirk must come before a vote on the kingdoms. The government very logically retorted that if the first vote went against union there would be no need to safeguard the Kirk.

At last the stalling had to stop. One of the twenty-six, William Seton the Younger of Pitmedden, rose to move the first article uniting the two kingdoms forever. According to Defoe, who was reporting everything to Harley, the English Secretary of State, the speech was very simply made, well-reasoned and without rhetoric. Seton rested the case on Scotland's desperate need of economic growth – through trade which would give access to the raw materials and markets of the new worlds in the east and west. Trade was impossible without the strength to protect it from competitors and enemies. These were England, France and Holland; Scotland must unite with one of them. Geography and the God of the Protestant religion had ordained that it must be England.

Lord Belhaven moved the rejection. He was another Hamilton, John by name, and had made a reputation as an orator in the Scottish parliament nearly twenty years earlier than the duke, having taken his seat in 1679 at the age of twenty-three on succeeding, like the duke, to a title which had come to him on petition and through a woman. His father had been a judge of the Court of Session and sat there as Lord Presmennan, but while still in his teens the son had married the grand-daughter of the first Lord Belhaven who, lacking another heir, obtained settlement of the title on his grand-daughter's husband. However, the favour did not dispose young Hamilton kindly towards Charles II's government and his highly critical orations in the parliament of 1681 so angered the Lord High Commissioner, James, Duke of York, that he consigned him to Edinburgh Castle to teach him to control his tongue. He was allowed to resume his seat when he consented to crave the royal pardon on his knees at the bar of the House. He enthusiastically embraced the Orange cause against James, commanded a troop of horse at Killiecrankie and was rewarded by being made a member of William's first Privy Council.

He had some talent for business as well as declamation, engaging in tax-farming as well as the agricultural kind, and was the author of one of the early efforts to persuade Scottish farmers to modernise their methods, a treatise entitled *An Advice to the Farmers of East Lothian to Labour and Improve their Grounds.* He had subscribed a thousand pounds to the Darien scheme and spoken long and loudly inside and outside parliament to commend it, and to castigate London rule when it failed. In 1704 his name was unjustly linked with those of the Dukes of Atholl and Hamilton in Simon Fraser's fabricated Jacobite plot. Whether this was Fraser's own malicious doing, or government agents were seizing an opportunity to discredit Belhaven, is not known. The two dukes were not above suspicion of conspiring with St Germains and Versailles but Belhaven ought to have been: his anti-government speeches were so clearly moved by nothing but a genuine love of his country and the Kirk. Tweeddale had won him over to the Squadrone Volante government by making him a commissioner of the treasury but he became a free man again when Argyll procured Tweeddale's dismissal and was now one of the most passionate and wholehearted opponents of union in the House. The twenty-six had hoped he would be among the progressive landlords who would see the benefits for themselves in union; they failed miserably to shake him out of his blazing nationalism. Lockhart of Carnwath saw him as 'a well-accom-plished gentleman in most kinds of learning, well-acquainted with the constitution of Scotland, and a skilful parliamentary strate-gist.' To pro-union John Macky, he was 'a rough, fat, noisy man, more like a butcher than a lord.' Lockhart's only complaint is of his 'long, premeditated harangues'. It was the most premeditated of these the House was now to hear.

He began by loudly extolling what her centuries of in-dependence had given Scotland – a free and proud people, a self-governing national church, a noble and honourable peerage, masters of their own lands and their own destinies since the days of the great Macallum More (a legendary ancestor of the Duke of Argyll). He switched to a gloomy vision of Scotland as she would be if she joined England.

'I think I see,' he cried 'a petty English exciseman receive more homage and respect than was formerly paid to Macallum More. I think I see the present peers of Scotland, whose noble ancestors conquered provinces, overran countries, reduced and subjected towns and fortified places, exacted tribute through the greatest part of England, walking in the Court of Requests like so many English attornies, laying aside their swords when in company with the English peers lest their self-defence should be found murder. I think I see the royal state of burghs walking their desolate streets, hanging down their heads under disappointments, wormed out of all the branches of their old trade, uncertain what hand to turn to, necessitated to become apprentices to their unkind neighbours, and yet after all finding their trade so fortified by companies and secured by prescriptions that they despair of any success therein. I think I see the honest, industrious tradesman, loaded with new taxes and impositions, disappointed of the equivalents, drinking water in place of ale, eating his saltless pottage, petitioning for encouragement to his manufactories and answered by counter-petitions. I think I see the laborious ploughman, with his corn spoiling upon his hands for want of sale, cursing the day of his birth, dreading the expense of his burial, and uncertain whether to marry or do worse. But above all I think I see our ancient mother Caledonia, like Caesar, sitting in the midst of our senate, ruefully looking about her, covering herself with her royal garment, attending the fatal blow and breathing out her last with an *et tu quoque, mi filii.*

'Our neighbours in England are not under the afflicting hand of Providence as we are. Their circumstances are great and glorious, their treaties are prudently managed at home and abroad, their generals brave and valorous, their armies successful and victorious, their trophies and laurels memorable and surprising, their enemies subdued and routed, their strongholds besieged and taken, sieges relieved, marshals killed and taken prisoners, provinces and kingdoms are results of their victories, the Royal Navy is the terror of Europe, their trade and commerce extended through the universe encircling the whole habitable world and rendering their own capital city the emporium for the whole inhabitants of the earth, and, which is yet more than all these things, the subjects freely bestowing their treasury upon their sovereign. And above all, these vast riches, the sinews of war, and without which all the glorious success has proved abortive, these treasures are managed with such faithfulness and nicety that they answer seasonably all their demands, though at never so great a distance. Upon these considerations how hard and difficult a thing will it prove to persuade our neighbours a self-denial bill.

'It is quite otherwise with us. We are an obscure, poor people, though formerly of better account, removed to a remote corner of the world, without name and without alliances, our ports mean and precarious so that I profess I do not think any one port of the kingdom worth the bringing after.'

Seton the Younger of Pitmedden no doubt smiled to hear his own case so unexpectedly supported by his opposer. Belhaven appealed to the government to recover its patriotism and abandon the treaty. His voice became a roar.

'Hannibal, my Lord Commissioner, is at our gates. Hannibal is come within our gates. Hannibal is come the length of this table. He is at the foot of this throne. He will demolish this throne. If we take not notice, he will seize upon these regalia. He will take them as our *spolia opima* and whip us out of this House, never to return again.'

He lowered himself down to his knees and stretched out his arms.

'I shall make a pause here till I see if His Grace my Lord Commissioner receive my humble proposals for removing misunderstandings among us. Upon my honour I have no other design and I am content to beg the favour on my bended knees.'

Receiving no response from Queensberry, he clambered to his feet again and denounced the commissioners for exceeding the mandate parliament had given them when they set out for London.

'Allow me to make this meditation. If our posterity after we are all dead and gone shall find themselves under an ill-made bargain and shall have recourse unto our records and shall see who have been the managers of this treaty, when they read the names they will certainly conclude and say: Ah, our nation has been reduced to the last extremity at the time of this treaty. All our great chieftains, all our great peers and considerable men who used formerly to defend the rights and liberties of the nation, have been killed and dead in the bed of honour before ever the nation was necessitated to condescend to such mean and contemptible terms. Where are the names of the chief men of the noble families of Stuarts, Hamiltons, Grahams, Campbells, Gordons, Johnstons, Homes, Murrays, Kerrs, et cetera? Where are the great officers of the Crown, the Constable and the Marischal of Scotland? They have certainly all been extinguished and now we are slaves for ever.'

There were a couple of Campbells, two Stuarts, and a Johnston among the commissioners listening to his lament.

'Whereas the English records will make their posterity reverence the memory of the honourable names who have brought under their fierce, warlike and troublesome neighbours who had struggled so long for independency, shed the best blood of their nation and reduced a considerable part of their country to become waste and desolate. When I consider this treaty I see the English constitution remaining firm, the same two Houses of Parliament, the same taxes, the same customs, the same excises, the same trade companies, the same municipal laws and courts of judicature, and all ours either subject to regulations or annihilations. Only we have the honour to pay their old debts and to have some few persons present for witnesses to the validity of the deed when they are pleased to contract more. Good God, what is this – an entire surrender!'

He stopped and tears rolled down his broad red face.

'My Lord, I find my heart so full of grief and indignation that I must beg pardon not to finish the last part of my discourse that I may drop a tear as the prelude to so sad a story.'

He slumped down and burst into wild sobbing.

When the surprised House recovered the Earl of Marchmont rose from the government benches. They had heard a long and terrible speech, he said, to which a short answer should suffice. 'Behold the noble lord dreamed,' he tartly observed, 'but lo when he awoke he found it was only a dream.'

A printed version of the speech from which these extracts have been taken was bought in large numbers and reverently read and re-read throughout Scotland for many years.

The question was put on the following day, November 4. Before the vote was taken the Duke of Atholl demanded that a formal protest against its legality should be entered in the record as 'contrary to the honour, interest, fundamental laws and constitution of this kingdom, the birthright of the peers, the rights and privileges of the counties and burghs, and contrary to the Claim of Right, property and liberty of the subjects.' He was supported by the Duke of Hamilton, one marquess, five earls, two viscounts, eight lords and forty-seven gentlemen.

The motion for approval of the first article ending the independence of Scotland was carried by one hundred and sixteen votes to eighty-three, a majority of thirty-three, a large number of the members abstaining. The 'yeas' consisted of the Duke of Argyll (the Duke of Queensberry, being Lord High Commissioner, did not vote), three marquesses, twenty-nine earls, two viscounts, eleven lords, thirty-seven representatives of counties and thirty-three representatives of burghs. The 'nays' were the Dukes of Hamilton and Atholl, one marquess, sixteen earls, two viscounts, thirty-three county and twenty-nine burgh representatives.

The first hurdle had been jumped. The twenty-six were getting their way.

As the government had promised, an act to secure 'the true Protestant religion' was introduced before the House rose, hushed with awe of what it had done. The Duke of Argyll had used all his military skill in disposing the troops and there was no rioting in Edinburgh that night. The mood was an appalled disbelief that the first step had been taken and a fierce conviction that something must happen to awake them from Belhaven's nightmare.

The opposition still fought hard, seeking anything that might yet keep the kingdoms apart. In the debate about the Kirk they thought they had found it. The English monarch swore an oath to defend the rights and privileges of the Church of England. How could this be squared with defence of the rights and privileges of the Kirk within a United Kingdom? English office-holders swore oaths of loyalty which inferred that they were willing to join in the sacraments of the Church of England. What about Scots who might be invited to take office in the new United Kingdom? Would Presbyterians be expected to bend the knee in an Episcopalian temple of Baal? The Kirk committee acting for the General Assembly was besieged by crowds braving the military and demanding answers to these knotty questions. It looked as if the pains the commissioners had taken to keep religious contention out of the treaty negotiations were to go for nothing. Answers would take months to get and could throw everything back into the melting pot, as the opposition intended. Union supporters in parliament knew the English had ways of getting round strict religious conformity when it suited them and would probably be willing to do so again. They were prepared to let the problems take care of themselves if the Kirk committee would be similarly easy-going. The arguments which had induced the committee members to opt for union in the first instance prevailed again. The opposition attack was fended off and the Kirk Act reached the statute book eight days after being introduced.

While this was happening Glasgow erupted.

There had been unrest in the town because the pro-union magistrates had refused to send a petition to parliament. After the news of the vote on the first article, the minister of the Tron Kirk preached a sermon in which he incautiously exhorted the congregation to 'up and be valiant for the city of God'. Interpreting this as a summons to action, they took to the streets with drums beating, and a mob of weavers, blacksmiths, shoemakers and butchers tried to force the Provost to sign a petition. When he escaped they seized a store of muskets and toured the town extorting signatures from the leading citizens for a petition which was despatched to Edinburgh under care of the deacons of the guilds of tailors and shoemakers. Tumult died down and the Provost came back. A man was arrested for offering one of the stolen muskets for sale. Afraid to start another riot, the Provost released him on a bond to appear again if required. Next day the mob, led by an ex-soldier and professed Jacobite called Finlay, demanded return of the bond. The Provost escaped again by concealing himself in a folding bed, from which he fled to Edinburgh. The other magistrates took refuge in the Tolbooth with the town guard and for several days the mob dominated the town. News of their rising had spread and reports came in of contingents offering to march from Lanarkshire, Stirling and as

E

far away as Angus. It was decided that they would assemble at Hamilton, the duke's own town in Lanarkshire, so a crowd set out from Glasgow armed with muskets and swords. An attempt by the magistrates to regain control of Glasgow resulted in a mutiny of the town guard and the mob captured the Tolbooth. Queensberry hurried off a couple of hundred dragoons from Edinburgh. When the Glasgow mob reached Hamilton the promised contingents from other towns and villages had not materialised, so they went back to Glasgow. Here the dragoons arrested Finlay, dispersed his followers, and took him off to the capital. Hardly were they out of the town before the mob re-assembled, beat the drums again, and forced the magistrates to despatch a delegation of baillies and deacons to Edinburgh to secure Finlay's release. Queensberry sent them home again to cope with the malcontents as best they could. Mob rule in Glasgow might be a nuisance to some of the citizens, but with Finlay under lock and key it was unlikely to menace the business the government had still to complete in Edinburgh.

Article Two brought Scotland into line with England over Hanover. Atholl and the Jacobites threw the full force of their oratory against it. Presbyterian opponents of union less confidently repeated the arguments for any king but England's. The vote followed the pattern of Article One. The Duke of Hamilton did not defect as some members of the government had predicted he would.

Over Article Three – one parliament – the opposition were making their next great stand. A vote for a separate Scottish parliament would effectively cancel out the two votes already taken. A single parliament was the *sine qua non* for England. They argued that Scotland, having so newly discovered the benefits and delights of genuine parliamentary debate about her own affairs, could not abandon them for a mere token partici-pation in discussion of English concerns, in which the Scottish members would be shouted down as impertinent interlopers if they ventured to interfere. They forecast that the United Kingdom would mean England and England alone to the English and to the world, and that Scotland would be dragged along at its tail like a led horse. They bemoaned the certainty that the English would glory in putting clamps on Scotland and forcing odious legislation on her, and that forty-five commoners and sixteen peers would be powerless to prevent them. They raised again the spectre of the bishops in the House of Lords and claimed it would be inconsistent with Presbyterian principles, the covenants of the past century, and the soul of the Kirk, to accept legislation in the making of which bishops had played any part.

Supporters of union were not entirely unmoved. Admittedly it was no old and revered institution whose demise was being discussed and it was easy to count more wreckers than real mourners among the opposition. There was substance, however, in the opposition's fears, as most privately admitted. Some had actually relished being members of a parliament in the last years and knew they were probably the first Scots to do so. They were grieved to be casting a vote to make this the last session of the Scottish parliament. If they could have had union and their own parliament too, they would have been genuinely relieved. Unhappily, England would not have a Scottish parliament and apparently Scotland could not live any more without England. It was sad but the Scottish parliament would have to go. The government majority went down, but Article Three was approved.

The mourners made one more try to keep a parliament alive in Scotland by moving next day that the United Kingdom parliament should meet at least once in every three years in Edinburgh. The government sidetracked by proposing that consideration be deferred until Article 22, dealing with Scottish representation in the London parliament. By the time that was reached the tears were dry and the proposal was forgotten.

One country, one king or queen, one parliament. Edinburgh roared in pain and rage, but Aryll's dragoons and footguards provided safe passage for all who needed it, and kept the hazards down to filth and stones.

Two days after the vote against a Scottish parliament something happened in the south-west. Two hundred members of the Cameronian sect of Presbyterian zealots marched into Dumfries, made a bonfire of the treaty in the market-place, and nailed a manifesto on the town cross. It declared that if the commissioners 'with their associates in Parliament shall presume to carry on the said union by a supreme power over the belly of the generality of this nation' it would not be binding on the people now or at any time to come. It called upon the government forces to have the spirits of Scotsmen and join with their fellow-countrymen in acquitting themselves as became men and Christians to forestall the treacherous plot to make them 'tributary and bondslaves to our neighbours' across the border. This might be the declaration of war Scotland was waiting for, and the secret agents Queensberry had placed where they were most likely to be needed moved in to carry out their briefing. Insinuating themselves among the Cameronians and finding that their leader was not as militantly inclined as his words suggested, they egged them on to take over the town, burn the houses of the few union supporters, and call out their sympathisers in the country round to march to Edinburgh. Rumours racing ahead of them to the capital spoke of five thousand men assembling on foot and two thousand on horseback. A march started with the secret agents in trusted positions in its van. When it was well out on the bleak road over the damp and windy hills and the marchers had had time to speculate on the discomforts and dangers lying ahead, the agents called a halt and delivered some startling news. They had all been tricked. It was not God or the Duke of Hamilton who marched unseen at their head but Satan himself. In their midst were secret emissaries of the Pope, conspirators from the Catholic courts of James Stuart and Louis of France. Invisible powers of darkness were in control and were leading them, not to free Scotland but to imperil the Kirk. The marchers were soon retracing their steps, loathing union as before but surer than ever that the devil was in everything, and that the safest way to escape him was to leave the world and Scotland to its predestined destruction and concentrate on thanking God for His wisdom and mercy in choosing them to be His elect.

Desperate minds in the capital started plotting assassination as well as shouting for it. One of the plots came to light in a letter sent to Queensberry by a conspirator who underwent an eleventh-hour change of heart. Twenty-two men had bound themselves by a horrid oath. 'Some of them are to be clothed in Highland dress, one in the habit of a beggar with a false beard, six are to be in the habit of baxters that by this means they may with the more ease raise the rabble. One of these in Highland dress is to stand on your left hand as you come out of the Parliament House with a naked dirk beneath his plaid to stab your Grace but if he has no opportunity for action then the beggar is to attend your coach with a pistol beneath his rags which he is to fire at your Grace, at which the baxters are to raise the rabble with their cries which they think will soon be done. . . . Perplexing thoughts so tormented me that I could neither sleep, eat or drink till I had eased my mind with this discovery. If your Grace will assure me of pardon I will come to your Grace's lodging and make a full discovery of this whole danger and let your Grace see their names written with their own hands and with their own blood for they put so much trust in me as that they gave it me in keeping.'

Nothing happened. The same paralysis afflicted would-be assassins as the rest of the population.

There was one indirect victim of the popular rage – Queensberry's scullion boy, the lowliest member of his household. Lord Drumlanrig, the Duke's heir, was a dangerous lunatic whom the family carried around with them, keeping him under guard in the cellars of their residences. One day a mob scuffled with the soldiers near the Queensberry town-house and the servants ran out to see the excitement, leaving the lunatic unguarded. Only the scullion stayed behind to watch a spit in the kitchen. Escaping from his cell, the madman killed the boy, stuck him on the spit and roasted him.

The debate in parliament dragged on through the rest of November, all December, and late into January, the opposition doggedly contesting every clause. Much of the argument was irresponsible. Impassioned demands were made, Defoe says, that Scots should be free from taxes nobody paid in England, that they should be safeguarded in liberties no Englishman had ever lost, and should enjoy as special rights and privileges equalities all England took for granted. The most was made of every point that could be raised in connection with food, drink, clothing, the means and the cost of living, since the adverse effect of union on these was the chief subject of discussion throughout the whole population.

Oats, Scotland's principle grain product and staple diet, was subjected to close comparison with wheat, of similar importance in England. When the price of English wheat fell below a certain level, dealers were encouraged to seek markets overseas by being allowed a 'drawback' of the duty levied on exports. There was no similar relief for the export of oats, which were not extensively grown in England. The opposition argued that Scots should enjoy an export bounty on oats similar to the bounty on wheat. The government replied that Scotland's principal trade in oats was with England and after union there would be no duty on which to claim a drawback. All the more reason, countered the opposition, why there should be a drawback for Scots if they were fortunate enough to sell oats to Holland or Germany or France. There was also alarm about cheap Irish oatmeal, which had hitherto been kept out of Scotland. It was allowed freely into England and under the union proposals it would have to be allowed equally freely into Scotland, to the ruin, it was argued, of Scottish growers and millers. The opposition moved a drawback on exported oats and oatmeal and a United Kingdom duty on imported oatmeal. Both government and opposition knew that however just these proposals might seem, they could delay, and possibly jeopardise, the treaty's acceptance by the English parliament. The government argued that the chief beneficiaries of a drawback on oats would be English dealers who would buy up all the Scottish oats they could lay hands on, export them to the continent, and collect the drawback for themselves. They reluctantly accepted a drawback for exported oatmeal and hoped Godolphin would be able to persuade the English parliament to accept it. They resisted a bounty for unground oats and a duty on Irish oatmeal.

The opposition did better, to their own discomfort, with salt. The pamphleteers had made great play with the dependence of Scots on salt for the curing of meat and fish, and foretold dire hardship to the poor if they had to pay the tax on salt levied in England. Under the treaty proposals, Scotland was to be exempted from this tax for seven years. The opposition spokesmen demanded perpetual exemption. The commissioners knew how they had vainly argued against the salt tax in London. So did the opposition, thanks to the inside information given them by George Lockhart of Carnwath. They hoped that if they could scare enough of the government's supporters with talk of starving people, unable to afford a mouthful of salt fish, they could secure a majority for an unlimited exemption, which England was sure to refuse, and the union would be wrecked. They painted their frightening pictures for two whole days, but the government scraped through. The opposers then returned to the attack with the argument that the terms of the treaty meant that after seven years the salt tax would automatically come into effect. An amendment should be made to prevent its imposition without further debate. The government pointed to the agreement that the tax would be imposed after the seven years only if the new United Kingdom parliament were satisfied that its imposition in Scotland would be to the benefit of the whole United Kingdom. This was greeted no doubt with mocking laughter from the other side but the amendment failed. It was clear to the government, however, that if they were to avoid the risk of an adverse vote at a later stage, when the more harrowing details of these salt discussions had spread throughout the country and members were reacting to the public anger, some concession would have to be made.

The English tax was levied in two parts. Two-thirds of its proceeds had been appropriated for ninety-nine years to assist the East India Company in the development and defence of its trade; the other third went to service the national debt and was collected under an arrangement due to expire in 1710. It was possible that by 1710 events might make the re-imposition of the one-third less necessary and so Scotland, with her seven-year exemption, might escape it altogether. The government proposed – no doubt after discreet soundings in London – that an amendment be made to exempt Scotland, after seven years, from the two-thirds of the tax collected for the benefit of the East India Company. At first sight this seems a strange amendment for Scotland to propose, in view of the importance the union advocates were attaching to trade. The East India Company operated a monopoly, however, and it was possible to argue – as the commissioners had failed to do in the original negotiations – that Scotland would derive no benefit from the company's trading and should therefore not be taxed for it. Two-thirds of the salt tax was an important concession for the government to make, particularly as there was at least a chance that the other third might lapse before it became applicable to Scotland. The opposition was taken aback by the move. They could claim two-thirds of a victory and say they had saved Scotland from complete starvation, but they had destroyed a vital element of their economic case against union if the amendment were acceptable to the English. They tried to fight back by declaring that the East India Company was not to be trusted: what they lost on the salt tax they would find another way of extorting from Scotland. The government promised that an addition to the Equivalent would be sought if anything so wicked should occur, and this soothing formula carried the day. The manoeuvre 'quietened public clamour', as Defoe puts it, and undoubtedly spiked a gun from which the opposition had expected explosive results.

They made nothing out of wool, but it was not for lack of trying. Raw Scottish wool was exported to France and other countries. The export of raw English wool was banned in the interest of cloth manufacture, and the Scots were expected to follow suit. Nobles and lairds in the Scottish borders made money out of the raw wool export trade and had frustrated efforts in the Scottish parliament to foster wool manufacture by copying the English practice. The opposition moved an amendment to the treaty freeing the export of raw wool from both countries, calculating that, if it were carried, the English would summarily reject it and the treaty would be sunk. They were defeated, so they moved a continuation of the export of Scottish wool. The government went to some trouble to demonstrate the absurdity of the proposal. It would require, they argued, the stationing of customs officers along the present border to prevent English traders from importing Scottish wool and re-exporting it, perhaps mixed with English wool. The officers would also have to prevent English wool from being smuggled into Scotland for re-export. Moreover, if English wool had to be kept out of Scotland to prevent its export, it would be impossible to use it in Scottish cloth manufacture and an industrial advantage of union would be lost. All ships sailing to and from Scottish ports would have to be searched to ensure that they carried no English wool into Scotland or Scottish wool into England. The searches would create animosities and there would be constant fighting between English and Scottish sailors. It was nonsense to unite for everything else and stay separate over wool. The disgruntled border woolmasters were reminded that wool manufacture could be subsidised out of the Equivalent and it was agreed to earmark £2 000 for that purpose.

An awkward circumstance affecting the cattle trade from Scotland into England was uncovered. Under the treaty this would be free of customs imposts. But the treaty preserved all the private rights of landowners, and an English family called Musgrave owned a border bridge over which the cattle passed to Carlisle. They exacted a toll. The cattle exporters argued that this toll was incompatible with free trade, and, as the free trade in cattle was one of the inducements the government had held out to their supporters, they had, rather uncomfortably, to give an undertaking to get this obstacle to union removed, hoping the English would be kind and find the way.

A tax on malt had been imposed in England to help to pay for the war with France. Malt was untaxed in Scotland and the treaty negotiators had agreed that it should remain so until such time as the new United Kingdom parliament should find it necessary to look again at the English tax. It was generally expected that the tax, which was highly unpopular in England, would be abolished as soon as the war should be over and the question of its imposition in Scotland would never arise. The opposition would not leave the matter there. They contended that the treaty must absolutely forbid a malt tax for the rest of time. All Scots were scared of the effect of malt taxes on the cost of their home-brewed ale and the government felt they must do something to mollify public opinion. They proposed that there should be no malt tax in Scotland for the duration of the war. Since thirsty Scots could not conceive of the Englishman, who also brewed ale at home, tolerating a tax on malt in time of peace, this amendment was seen as a marked improvement on the earlier wording and a victory for the watchdogs of the Scottish national interest.

Ale sold in inns and ale-houses was taxed in both countries, but the English tax was higher than the Scottish tax. Since the English tax could hardly be adjusted downwards, in view of the country's heavy and rising expenditure, the Scottish tax would have to be raised. The opposition protested that Scottish ale was weaker than English ale and so Scots should pay less tax. Again the government felt a concession was politic. A committee was set up which – with some help from himself, Defoe claims – found a formula acceptable to the English treasury and the brewers.

A question repeatedly raised was whether it would not be better for the Scots to keep their independence and to develop trade with France instead of England. Another committee was set up and, after hearing all the available evidence, reported that most of the English rates of duty on food and on articles in general use were lower than the Scottish rates and that, contrary to the opposition argument that prices would rise intolerably and the poor be further impoverished, the new terms on which trade would be carried on should be to the advantage of all sections of the population. They admitted that imports from France would be dearer, but pointed out that these were luxury articles – wine, brandy, silk, glass, fruit, fine clothes, hats, toys – bought only by the more well-to-do, and argued that everybody would benefit if the higher duties encouraged home manufacture of some of the articles, as had happened in England. Scotland's balance of trade with France had always been heavily disadvantageous. Twice as much per annum could be gained by trade with England as was being lost every year in trade with France.

The Equivalent was denounced as a wholly inadequate solatium for shouldering the English national debt. In a year, it was declared, Scots would have paid back to England through increased taxation the total amount of the Equivalent and so for-ever after would be paying off twenty million pounds of English debt they had no hand in incurring. Taxpayers would derive no benefit from distribution of the Equivalent unless they were crown creditors or Darien investors. The government spokesmen appealed to logic: Scotland wanted equality of trading oppor-tunity; equality of trade demanded equality of taxation, other-wise English traders would face ruin from unfair Scottish competition; the English could not service their national debt without drawing on the proceeds of taxation; therefore, if the Scots wanted equality of trade, they had to accept a share in the servicing of a national debt which would hereafter be a United Kingdom national debt. Defoe says this was 'the hardest thing in the world' to make Scots apprehend. Members of the opposition understood well enough, he declares, but used it 'as a handle to rally the rabble'.

Even the proposal that the Equivalent should be used to reimburse losses on the Darien scheme, which the treaty negotiators had believed would make a powerful appeal in the country, was opposed. Why dissolve the Africa Company? Why not keep it in being and use the Equivalent to help it compete with the East India Company? The government easily disposed of this suggestion. The company's shares had only been partly paid up and considerable sums were still on call. Many of the original investors had sold their shares for trifling sums to avoid having to meet a call. There was no support anywhere for keeping the company alive, only hands held out for any Equivalent money that might be going.

It had been foreseen during the treaty negotiations that a difficulty would arise if English coinage were adopted in Scotland. Scots shillings would have to be exchangeable without loss for English shillings. But Scots who now held English shillings could exchange them for thirteen Scots pence. These would consider they were suffering a loss under a straightforward substitution of English for Scots money. It had therefore been agreed by the treaty negotiators that such losses would be recompensed out of the Equivalent. The opposition found an alarming snag in this proposal. What, they asked, will prevent Englishmen from swarming over the border with saddle-bags full of English shillings and collecting a penny out of the Equivalent for every one of them? By this trick, they maintained, it would be possible for the English to take the full amount of the Equivalent back again, leaving nothing at all for the crown creditors, or the Darien investors, or to start a wool industry and recompense the raw wool exporters for their losses. Even in its immediate cash benefits the union would turn out to be a swindle. The government could not abandon the scheme because the holders of English money, who stood to get an immediate bonus out of union, included members of parliament on whom they were relying for votes. But the danger threatened by the opposition would have to be obviated. They had recourse again to a committee. In an age when the fastest means of communication was a man on horseback the committee's solution may well have been the best that could be found. They suggested that a date should be fixed on which all Scots possessing English coins should bring them to places where they would be counted, sealed, and returned with a certificate of entitlement to payment out of the Equivalent. The date should be kept secret until all the arrangements had been made and announced with sufficient time for Scots to reach the appointed places, but not enough for Englishmen to get there, unless they happened to live very close to the border.

A fruitless attempt was made to save Scots from being lifted by press-gangs for service in the English – soon to be British –

navy. It was moved that they should be exempt for seven years and that thereafter the number of Scots who could be forced into service should be in the same proportion to the United Kingdom total as the Scottish tax yield bore to the total yield, this ratio being unalterable by any future parliament. The point was made in reply that press-gangs should not be needed to find Scots for the navy, since so many Scots had volunteered for service in the Danish, Swedish and Dutch navies. Free press-ganging, the government declared, was inseparable from free trade.

Among the rights which the treaty was to leave intact was the privilege of burghs to continue to levy local taxes in existence at the time of union, for public works of various kinds. These needed parliamentary approval, and since this would be the last opportunity to get the approval of a Scottish parliament if the treaty went through, burghs hurried to push through new imposts while there was still time. Town halls and prisons, harbours, bridges and piers were suddenly discovered to be urgent necessities, and in spite of the opposition's fear of the perpetual thirst union would inflict on the Scots, the taxes were all on ale and wine. The votes of burgh representatives were important, so the government made time for the measures. Dundee sought twopence on the pint of ale. It may have been a member with a sad feeling that an old order was passing away, or a joker, who moved the condition that the town pay part of the proceeds for six years to Mr James Anderson, a lawyer, to enable him to search after antiquities. Laughing or weeping, the House agreed.

Winter was not as severe as the government had hoped. A motion banning all public gatherings was carried on December 27.

Article 22 was reached on January 8. It fixed the representation Scotland was to have in the United Kingdom parliament at sixteen peers in the Lords and forty-five members in the Commons, and it was the opposition's final chance of obstructing the treaty. If they could persuade the House that a proportion of something under one Scot to ten Englishmen was an insult, negotiations would have to be reopened and anything might happen. It was agreed, however, that if the effort should fail the Duke of Hamilton would make a grand outburst and lead all the members who were prepared to follow him out of the House and into the street, never to return. They would march down the High Street, daring the troops to stop them, and the walk-out would be the signal for revolution which the nation was awaiting.

The plot revived the opposition's flagging spirits, and the debate began in a crowded and emotion-charged House. The opposition case was the seemingly reasonable one that representation of the two countries in the new United Kingdom parliament should be based on common principles. If the English wanted all their present membership to be continued, the entire present Scottish membership should also be continued. If the English insisted on cutting down Scottish representation, English representation should be reduced on whatever principles had been applied to determine the Scottish numbers. Members noted that the Duke of Hamilton was not in his place and a messenger was sent to inquire about him. He returned with the shattering news that the duke had decided not to appear that day because he had toothache. A delegation went off to protest. Even if he made no speech he must lead the walk-out. Eventually they brought him back with them to the chamber.

The government's defence of the treaty proposals was made by John Dalrymple, Earl of Stair, reputed to be the best speaker in the House. Stair was not liked by Scots, but in entrusting him with the reply to the opposition attack on this crucial article of the treaty, Queensberry was acknowledging that, as Lockhart also admitted, 'there was none in Parliament capable to take up the cudgels with him.' He was an advocate and had at one time been popular with the masses because of the persecution to which he had been subjected by Charles II's government following his eloquent defence of the Earl of Argyll in his first treason trial in 1681. He was imprisoned, fined, and made to apologise for his lenient treatment of covenanting tenants on his family estates; later he was arrested again and confined to Edinburgh on bail of £5 000. James II charged his father with treason, and it seems likely his estates would have been forfeited, had not the son paid a visit to London and returned to Edinburgh with a remission of the charges against his father, a sum of money to cover his own fines and losses, and the post of Lord Advocate, from which his predecessor had been dismissed for refusing to exercise the royal prerogative in pro-Catholic ways he considered illegal. This sudden change of front reversed the esteem Dalrymple had been building up and in a few years he was hated by every Presbyterian. He claimed later that he had gone over to James to be in a better position to help William of Orange. William was willing to believe him and gave him high office in his first Scottish administration. But the country was not prepared to forgive him. Parliament refused to approve taxation unless William assented to an act they passed which would have forced Dalrymple's dismissal. William decided he would do without Scottish money, prorogued parliament, and retained Dalrymple. His enemies fell out among themselves, however, and the dispute between parliament and the king blew over. Dalrymple began to court the Presbyterians by helping the Kirk to recover from some of the depredations of Charles and James, and he was on the way back to popular favour when the Macdonalds were massacred at Glencoe.

He had persuaded William to offer an indemnity to rebel clans if they took an oath of allegiance before January 1, 1692. His aim was to pacify the Highlands, but he hoped some of the clansmen would refuse the offer and be so severely punished 'by fire and sword and all manner of hostility', as he phrased it, that no Highlander would rebel in future. When the chief of the Macdonalds found no one at Fort William to administer the oath to him on December 31, and so succeeded in taking it at Inverlochy only on January 6, Dalrymple would not forego the bloody example he had planned and the massacre took place. Public anger over its treacherous manner gave his parliamentary enemies the opportunity to attack him again. They had to move carefully because of the involvement of the king in the affair, but when an inquiry absolved him from personal responsibility for the behaviour of the soldiers and fixed the blame on the troop commander, they voted an address to William that his minister had also exceeded the royal instructions and should be removed from office. Dalrymple saved William from having to accede to the request by resigning all his posts. Succession to his father's peerage as Viscount Stair in 1695 gave him a parliamentary seat again but he made no attempt to claim it until later that year when parliament admitted he had no advance knowledge of the method the troop commander used in carrying out the punishment order, and so could have had no responsibility for the more horrible aspects of the massacre. Members nevertheless received him with such hostility when he appeared in the House that he stayed away for five years. When parliament accepted him in 1700, Anne did something towards rehabilitating him by creating him an earl and giving him a privy councillorship. He had also been selected to take part in the union negotiations. In the current session of parliament he had used all his eloquence and skill in debate as a private member to put the union measure through. For three months he had worked night and day, expounding, exposing, entreating, intriguing. The opposition reviled him and Lockhart denounced him as the Judas of Scotland. He seems genuinely to have believed that the union was in the best interests of the Scottish people and spared himself in no way to effect it. He was sixty and showing signs of strain, but that afternoon he made one of the speeches of his career.

His argument was that talk of principle would get Scotland nowhere. The only facts known for certain about the two countries which provided any basis for comparison concerned their revenues. The English would begin by paying into the union treasury thirty-eight times as much as the Scots. They could justifiably maintain that they were entitled to thirty-eight times as many members. Scots ought to consider themselves lucky to get one to ten. When he sat down he had convinced all but the hard core of the opposition that the English had done them proud. The article was carried by forty votes.

All eyes on the opposition side turned immediately to Hamilton. Now was the moment for the signal that was to bring the clans down from the hills and glens, the lowlanders from their fields and workshops, and sweep government, parliament and union into the North Sea. They looked in vain. With his hand to his face the duke sat glumly nursing his aching tooth. The government leaders and supporters began to hurry from the chamber, and the opportunity for a dramatic gesture had passed. The inexplicable duke had let them down again.

Tragic news awaited the House when it assembled next morning. The eloquent Stair had been found dead in his bed. The doctors said it was sheer exhaustion, or possibly an apoplectic fit. The town when they heard of it said it was a judgement of God on him. Either that or he had committed suicide from remorse for the terrible thing he had done to Scotland.

On January 14 the last article was approved and on

January 16 the whole treaty was re-presented as an act and passed by one hundred and ten votes to sixty-nine, a majority of forty-one. Queensberry touched it with the sceptre. 'Now there's an end of an old song,' remarked Lord Chancellor Seafield as he handed the documents to the clerk. There was a chuckle in his voice, it is said, and presumably no tears in his eyes.

Hamilton bobbed up again on the last day. As Queensberry was picking up the sceptre a spokesman for the Duke of Douglas, who was too young to speak for himself, rose to object to union taking away his hereditary right to lead the van of the army of Scotland into battle against the English. Hamilton jumped up to object to the objection. That right, he declared, belonged to him. Opposition members groaned, jeered and cursed. When they had looked for his pennant to lead them into battle all they had seen was a handkerchief raised to his jaw. He had replaced Queensberry as their greatest hate.

By March 4 the treaty had passed both Houses of the English parliament. The minor Scottish amendments were accepted and the awkward business of the toll charge for Scottish cattle crossing the bridge near Carlisle was overcome by parliament agreeing to buy out the ancient Musgrave family rights. Not all the English were glad to take the Scots to their bosoms. The High Tories denounced the recognition of the right of Scots to their own religion, and deplored the admission of Presbyterian feet to the sanctified pavements of Westminster. The Earl of Nottingham declared that the terms of the union destroyed the constitution of England. Scotland had been treated far too generously and the payment of the Equivalent was a needless burden on an England already staggering under the cost of the French war. Sixteen peers were too many in the House of Lords and their votes would have consequences that could not be foreseen. But Godolphin's Whig and moderate Tory supporters knew that what he had wanted and was getting was the key of the back-door to button tightly in England's pocket, and were solidly with him on every clause. The bishops quickly got together an act to protect the Church of England from the Presbyterians, to set beside the Scottish act preserving the Kirk from episcopal intrusions, and with this on the statute book it was felt that if no great good was to be expected from the Scots they could not do much harm. The

Archbishop of Canterbury graciously declared he thought the Kirk as truly Protestant as the Church of England, if not so perfect.

On March 6 Queen Anne touched the English Act of Union and announced: 'I desire and expect from all my subjects of both nations that from henceforth they act with all possible respect and kindness to one another that so it may appear to all the world that they have hearts disposed to become one people.'

The Scottish parliament sat on to wind up its affairs and decide who should go to Westminster. The government proposed that the new representatives should be elected by and from the existing membership. Hamilton laboured on in his role of lost leader of the van. He demanded a general election for the forty-five commoners. He had his speech printed and carried all over the country. It started up some shouting again but the masses remained in the trauma into which the loss of their nationhood had thrust them. The duke's plea was bluntly rejected. He proposed that peers created in the last thirty years should relinquish the right to sit in parliament and give way to the ancient nobility, of which he was unquestionably one. Defeated, he fell back on a scheme of rotation beginning with the oldest creations and was turned down again. The sixteen peers were elected by the peers in the House from among themselves and neither Hamilton nor any other noble opposer of union was among them. It was agreed that the burghs, arranged in groups, should have fifteen representatives and the counties, also with some groupings, thirty. Grouped constituencies should appoint commissioners to elect one of their existing representatives. It worked out in favour of the pro-unionists as the government desired. Lockhart of Carnwath was not chosen this time, of course, but at a general election a year later he won a seat at Westminster to play a lively part in the events of the next chapter.

One of the last acts of the House was to recommend William Paterson to Queen Anne for 'his good service' in helping to draft the trade and finance articles of the Treaty of Union and calculating the Equivalent. The recommendation was made to ease consciences. Paterson had been paid two hundred pounds for his work for the treaty commissioners but a very large sum of money, which he should have obtained out of the part of the Equivalent allotted to reimburse Darien investors, had inadver-

G

tently been overlooked. The Equivalent had been fixed by the treaty down to a very precise ten shillings and all who had claims on it were unwilling to see the allocations disturbed to make room for Paterson in case they might be worse off in consequence. So parliament recommended Paterson to the attention of the queen in the hope that she would find a way of being more generous to him than his fellow-Scots felt able to be.

The Scottish parliament met for the last time on March 25. The final words were spoken by Queensberry:

'My Lords and Gentlemen,

'The public business of this session being now over, it is full time to put an end to it. I am persuaded that we and our posterity will reap the benefit of the union of the two kingdoms, and I doubt not that, as this Parliament has had the honour to conclude it, you will in your personal stations recommend to the people of this nation a grateful sense of her Majesty's goodness and great care for the welfare of her subjects in bringing this important affair to perfection, and that you will promote an universal desire in this kingdom to become one in hearts and affections, as we are inseparably joined in interest, with our neighbour nation.

'My Lords and Gentlemen,

'I have a very deep sense of the assistance and respect I have met with from you in this session of Parliament, and I shall omit no occasion of showing, to the utmost of my power, the grateful remembrance I have of it.'

With almost as much indecent haste as King James VI, Queensberry set out on a triumphal progress to London which nearly paralleled the jamboree of a hundred and four years earlier. He didn't hunt and he didn't make knights or distribute borrowed money but there were cheers and junketing in plenty once he was over the border. The north of England was happy to think there would be no more Scots invasions, although the cheering on that score was a little premature, as they found in 1715 and 1745. Queensberry sat down to a banquet in every town of any size, and at Barnet the queen's ministers and members of the House of Lords came out to meet him with forty-six coaches and over a thousand horses. Londoners threw their hats in the air. For the first time since James, a Scot entering London was made to

feel welcome. James brought only himself. Queensberry deserved
a triumph. He brought a captive kingdom.

On May 1 the treaty of union came into effect. England and
Scotland were formally united. The United Kingdom of Great
Britain was born. England took a holiday. Scotland spent the day
in anguished mourning. Thirty-one great whales committed
suicide by beaching themselves on the coast of Fife and Scots far
beyond the smell of the rotting carcases saw the unnatural and
unaccountable event as a grim omen of worse disasters to come.
Queen Anne, attended by her lords, gentlemen and ladies in
four hundred coaches, drove to St Paul's and gave thanks from
her entirely English heart for the greatest of the victories with
which God had blessed her reign.

10 A Surrender to Destiny

Six years later the union almost broke up. An effort in the House of
Lords to separate England and Scotland again and for ever was
frustrated by four votes. Argyll, Seafield and Mar voted for it,
as did all the Whigs who had put union through the English
parliament. Queensberry would probably have voted for it too,
had he still been alive.

Controversy began even before union was formally effected.
The duties on brandy and wine imported into Scotland were
lower than the English duties. English merchants who brought
tobacco into England paid a duty of sixpence a pound, but if they
re-exported it to Scotland they got fivepence back. When the treaty
was signed by the commissioners, merchants in both countries
saw the chance of making some easy money if the duties were
brought into line. Scots put all the cash they could raise into
buying brandy and wine from France with the intention of making
a profit on selling it in England if union went through. English
traders rushed tobacco over from America and pushed it into
Scotland, recovering their fivepences and meaning to bring it
back into England if union went through.

London wine merchants objected to the prospect of being
undersold by the Scots after May 1 and lobbied for a bill, which
was duly presented in the English House of Commons to prevent
'this fraudulent practice'. The English customs authorities protested loudly at being robbed of revenue from both sides when the
border barriers were dismantled. The bill to frustrate the knavish
tricks was enthusiastically passed by the Commons. The Scots
traders sent up a howl. They had been told free trade would
turn out to be a fraud. Here was proof. As soon as they had an
opportunity of making money the English parliament was balking
them of it. It was exactly what the opposition were saying they
could expect from union.

The Whig Lords, nervous lest the Scots masses be provoked to revolt, threw out the Commons bill on the ground that the English parliament had no right to make a unilateral interpretation of articles of the treaty. The Commons sent the bill back again. The Lords stuck to their point. It was better, a member said, to let wine merchants grumble than to disgust a kingdom and the best of queens by endangering the constitution of the new Great Britain. The Commons gave up but not the customs authorities. Six weeks after the union took effect forty ships from Scotland, laden with wine, brandy and tobacco, arrived in the Thames and were boarded by customs officers. The cargoes might not be dutiable, they declared, but the wines and the brandies were forfeit. They came from France, with which the new Great Britain was at war. The hullabaloo broke out again. The goods had not come from France, protested the Scots, they were from Scotland and Scotland was not at war with France until May 1. The Lords were still disposed to handle Scotland with care, so at its first sitting the United Kingdom parliament voted to release the ships and tell the customs people to hold their peace for the sake of the new nation.

The kid gloves were not long in coming off, however. Some Scots were arrested for treasonable dealings with the French and tried in a Scots court and under Scots law. The English thought they were too leniently punished, and in 1709 parliament, heedless of the protests of the Scottish members that such action was in blatant disregard of the article of the treaty preserving Scots law, passed an act to bring the Scots treason law and procedure into line with the English. As English members saw it, they were stopping up a hole in the security arrangements which were the reason for union. The Scots viewed their action as a serious breach of the treaty provisions.

In 1710 Queen Anne dismissed Godolphin and replaced him with Tory ministers. On their advice she forgave the Duke of Hamilton his opposition to union and made him Duke of Brandon. Hamilton thought this should give him a seat in the House of Lords as a peer of the United Kingdom. The English Lords objected and passed a measure which debarred a peer of the United Kingdom from sitting in parliament if he had been a peer of Scotland at the time of the union. This unseated not only Hamilton but also Queensberry, who had been created Duke of

Dover as a reward for his part in putting through the union. The Scottish nobility were enraged. They had looked forward to United Kingdom peerages as a means of securing seats in the Lords without having to be one of the elected sixteen. Now they were being reduced to a second-class status among United Kingdom peers.

The new parliament also upset the Kirk. In 1709 Edinburgh magistrates had imprisoned an Episcopalian clergyman for refusing to obey the General Assembly's injunction against his English prayer-book. He appealed unsuccessfully to the Court of Session, then to the House of Lords, thus raising the question of the jurisdiction of that body as an appeal court which the treaty commissioners had left unsettled. The House decided in 1711 in its favour. This was bad enough as another invasion of Scotland's right to her own courts of law, but the House went on to free the clergyman, overriding not only the magistrates of the Scottish capital but also the supremacy in spiritual matters of the Kirk itself. Nor did parliament stop there. In quick succession in 1712 it passed acts legalising the Episcopal Church in Scotland, restoring the right of landowners to appoint ministers to parishes in defiance of the Kirk's practice of congregational election, and establishing a Christmas holiday for the law courts, which to Presbyterians was letting the Pope put his toe in the door.

Scots who could afford French wines and brandy had another grievance. Smuggling to evade the ban on dealing with the enemy was a popular pastime in both countries, but it was a new idea to the Scots that they were at war with France, and English customs officers were sent into Scotland to keep their Scots colleagues up to scratch and teach them English standards and methods. The Englishmen were the physical evidence of conquest which Lord Belhaven had luridly anticipated in his famous speech. Mobs stoned them, and high and low thought it both a human right and a patriotic duty to frustrate them. The Englishmen compounded their villainy by working on the Sabbath. When the Equivalent turned up it was found to be half paper money, a novelty to most Scots, who considered they had been cheated. Everything the Scots had feared, everything the opponents of union had predicted, seemed to be happening, and Scotland's parliamentary representatives were powerless to prevent it. Belhaven's horrible dream had come true: Hannibal was indeed within the gates.

The Scottish members were not united in resisting the out-rages. Peers deserted the Kirk to enjoy the privileges of patronage and Jacobite Lockhart of Carnwath revelled in putting the Episcopal cat among the Presbyterian pigeons. But by the summer of 1713 the anger at home had mounted so high that they were impelled to present a unanimous demand for repeal of the union acts.

It will be remembered how exercised the Scots had been during the Treaty of Union debates lest malt should be taxed in Scotland as it was in England, and that the terms of the treaty had been amended to rule the possibility out so long as the United Kingdom remained at war. In the spring of 1713 it was clear that the War of the Spanish Succession was all but over. The Tory government had rid themselves of Marlborough, following Godolphin's dismissal by Anne, and he was in virtual exile in Holland; they had arranged an armistice with the French and withdrawn the British army to fresh lines to force their Dutch and Austrian allies to join in negotiating peace. The war did not formally end until the Treaty of Utrecht was signed at the end of March, but the government were so anxious not to lose the revenue from the English malt tax, due to expire with the war, that they passed a new tax through parliament several weeks before the peace was signed and applied it at the rate of sixpence a bushel to the whole United Kingdom. The patience of the Scots had been sorely strained by the successive breaches, according to their interpretation, of the letter or the spirit of the Treaty of Union. It had almost broken with the imposition in 1711 of a duty on linen sent abroad. Linen was their chief contribution to the United Kingdom's export trade and the treaty had expressly provided that in imposing new taxes parliament should have 'due regard to the circumstances and abilities of every part of the United Kingdom'. The malt tax broke their patience completely. They had believed that a tax on malt in peace-time was impossible, even in England. They had been assured the English would not stand for it. They had imagined they were safe from it for ever when they had averted its application to themselves while the war lasted. Now, when the war was to all intents and pur-poses finished, when all that remained was to sign and seal the peace treaty, it had been clamped upon them. Their fury at the scoundrelly behaviour, as they saw it, of the English members of parliament was understandable. They were spitting on the treaty and insulting and affronting the whole Scottish nation. Their protests in parliament having been in vain, the Scottish peers and commoners had no option but to combine in an effort to win back Scotland's independence – if they wished to safeguard their lives and property from the indignation of the mobs.

They decided to move for leave to bring in a bill to repeal the Acts of Union. They knew the motion had no chance if its success depended on Scots votes. Scotland was imprisoned in the union so long as a majority of the English members of either House of parliament were determined to keep her there. It happened, however, that there was at that juncture no certainty of such determination. The Scots made no secret of their intention and the pros and cons of repeal were soon being openly discussed by all the party factions. The Tories, who had a majority in both houses, were badly divided. The Earl of Oxford, formerly Robert Harley, leader of the pro-Godolphin moderate Tories in the Commons, was now Lord High Treasurer, Anne's chief minister, and nominal head of the party. He was emphatically opposed to repeal. He believed sincerely that it was in the interest of both countries to preserve the union. He had also a more personal reason for opposing repeal. The Jacobites in his party, led by Henry St John, later Viscount Bolingbroke, saw the separation of the two kingdoms as a breach in the legislation intended to secure the succession of the House of Hanover, which could be enlarged, when Anne died, into an opening for the return of her half-brother across the water. St John was bold and impetuous, Oxford cautious and hesitant. In Oxford's view the time was not yet ripe for any dramatic improvement of the Pretender's prospects. It was also essential for the maintenance of his own position in the party that St John's hopes in this matter of repeal should not be realised. Oxford could muster a small majority for his view within the party but this could not help him if a combination of all the Scots and St John's Jacobites received any substantial support from the Whigs. The Whigs had put the union through the English parliament against Tory opposition. Unhappily for Oxford, there was a distinct possibility that, six years later, they were willing to see their work undone. Their chief reason for backing the union of the parliaments had been to lock the back-door into England against the French. This seemed to be less important when peace was being made with the French. Their one concern now was to revenge themselves on the Tories for making the peace against their wishes, by embarrassing them in every way in parliament, and inflicting a resounding defeat on them in the next general election, which could not long be deferred. Their support for the Scottish motion would force Oxford to use all his ingenuity to compel his party to stand together in awkward defence of the union they had formerly opposed, or to face a humiliating defeat by the Whigs in alliance with his enemies within his party. Whatever might happen to the motion, the Whigs stood to gain in the general election, for the union had won no popularity among English voters. If the motion succeeded and Scotland were on her own again, it would do no harm for Scots to be grateful to an English Whig government. If the motion failed, Scots would still think well of Whigs and support them in the election and in parliament after it. The whole Whig party was in the grip of a blatant anti-Tory cynicism in which only one shred of principle survived: their attachment to the Hanover succession. They informed the Scots that, if they would agree to insert a clause preserving the Hanover succession in the bill for the dissolution of the union, they would vote solidly for it. The stipulation was no comfort to Oxford. It would disconcert St John if it were accepted by the Scots, but it would still leave open the possibility of a Tory defeat.

The Scots were divided about the Whig condition. Lockhart of Carnwath had been the chief promoter of the motion but he was reluctant to have repeal on the Whigs' terms. Hanover supporters had no objection to giving the Whigs the assurance they sought, if they would not thereby be ensuring the return of Scotland to an independence at least half of them did not want. They had been willing enough to play to the angry gallery at home by making a vigorous demonstration in favour of repeal but were thoroughly alarmed now there was a probability that they might succeed. Tory Oxford sent for Scottish Tory Lockhart and tried to persuade him to drop the motion, which might be so advantageous to the Whigs and could do no good to the Jacobite cause. 'You will bring an old house about your ears and the queen will highly resent your conduct,' he warned the Scot. 'We cannot well be worse than we are. We must now make the best of a bad bargain,' Lockhart records his reply. Oxford stormed. Lockhart should expect nothing of any ministry with which he had any influence. Lockhart shrugged. 'Discouragement is no new thing,' he answered sourly. 'You will find us all the more resolute for your threats. If it be needful, we have the courage to suffer for our country.'

Lockhart was eager to start the process of asking for leave to introduce the bill in the Commons, where it was certain to pass with forty-five Scots to vote for it, in addition to Whigs and St John Tories. The Duke of Argyll was determined that the first step should be taken in the Lords, where there were only sixteen Scottish votes, Oxford would be able to speak, and the outcome was less predictable. Supported by other worried Scots, the duke got his way and on June 1, 1713, ex-Scottish Lord Chancellor Seafield, now Earl of Findlater, moved for leave to introduce a repeal bill. The Earl of Mar followed, and later Argyll. Lord Somers, the English lawyer who had written much of the Treaty of Union, spoke formally for the motion on behalf of the Whigs. It was soon evident, however, that there was confusion in the Whig ranks. Either by intent or inadvertence, the Scots had brought in their motion without first giving the Whig leadership a formal and binding answer to the question about the succession which they had asked. Members of the party were uncertain how to speak. Oxford saw his opportunity. He moved that the question be put without further debate. Objections were raised by some who sought time to have the position of the Scots clarified, but Oxford's motion was carried by four votes. 'Thereafter', says Duncan Forbes of Culloden, then beginning his political association with the Duke of Argyll and so a very interested observer, 'the question was put whether leave should be given to bring in the bill or not, and it carried in the negative by a vast majority, all the Whigs voting against it because it was proposed out of concert before they had time to prepare it.' A correspondent reported the scene to Dean Swift: 'It was very comical to see the Tories, who voted with the Lord Treasurer against the dissolution of the union, under all the perplexities in the world lest they should be victorious; and the Scotch, who voted for the bill of dissolution, under agonies lest they themselves should carry the point.' The last remark may be unjust to some of the Scots but no more was heard of the repeal proposal. Despite his brave words to Oxford, Lockhart did not try to introduce it in the Commons.

He was genuinely disappointed at the failure of the effort but there were compensations. He enjoyed being a Scottish Puck among the English politicians and opportunities of furthering his Jacobite objectives would no doubt come soon.

For the next fifty years the Scots continued to groan and grieve, convinced that they had been laid under an evil spell from which some day and somehow they would be released. They believed for a time the magic used must have been bribery, that the votes which had delivered them into captivity in 1707 had been bought. There seemed grounds for the belief.

It became known that in October 1706, a week or two before the first vote on union, £20 000 arrived in Edinburgh from the English Treasury. The payment was unusual and the circumstances suspicious. The money had been consigned, not to the Scottish Treasury, but to Commissioners of the Treasury personally, and had been signed for by them in their personal capacities. There was no doubt it had been distributed to men who had voted for union. Lockhart of Carnwath produced a list of thirty-two of them, one short of the number by which the first vote for the treaty was carried. Could anything, the Scots told themselves, be more convincing and damning? Scotland had been sold for a miserable £20 000 doled out to thirty-two contemptible creatures who had sacrificed the freedom of a million of their countrymen to stow away a few hundred gold pieces each. The tale of the scandal grew to such proportions that in 1711 it had to be investigated by United Kingdom Commissioners of Public Accounts. The report exonerated the English government of procuring or aiding corruption but did little to cure the Scots of their conviction that they were its victims. The money had been sent, it was said, to allow the crown to discharge its debts for services performed in its Scottish kingdom before that kingdom should be swallowed up in a new United Kingdom. Some of these debts were very old and it was not unreasonable that the creditors wished to have them honoured before they dealt with the creation of circumstances which might give the crown an excuse for shuffling out of its obligations. The Scottish Treasury had been short, so the English Treasury advanced the money and the debts were discharged : £12 325 to Queensberry for expenses as Lord High Commissioner, £1 104 to the Earl of Marchmont (who had accused Belhaven of dreaming after his passionate speech) for expenses incurred when he had been Lord Chancellor, and to 25 others sums ranging down to £11 2s. Among these was the Duke of Atholl, who got £1 000.

Historians, Scots and English, now accept that most of the money was used to meet outstanding debts. Queensberry had been asking for years to have his expenses paid. Marchmont complained of hundreds owing to him as far back as 1702. Only an idiot optimist could have expected to swing Atholl's vote to union for £1 000 and others are unlikely to have been content with between £1 000 and £11 when Queensberry was getting £12 000. It is thought that some of the money may have brought a few switherers down off the fence on the right side (votes were bought on both sides of the border in those days) and that some may have taken advantage of the situation by claiming and being paid debts already discharged. Public accounts were not scrupulously kept in the early eighteenth century and the exchequer was considered fair game. But over half the peers who voted for union were crown office-holders or pensioners and any of them may have had genuine unpaid claims. The fact remains that the money was paid out at a highly suspicious moment and the Scots, who badly needed some way of explaining to themselves the calamity that had befallen them, cannot be blamed for catching at this one.

The real explanation, which they did not begin to grasp until well into the second half of the century, was that they had in truth been under a spell when they had failed so miserably to stop the twenty-six from handing over their independence to the English – the spell of a destiny they were then incapable of recognising.

The Scots were not by nature weak and ineffective or slow to assert themselves. Whenever the occasion had required it in the past they had readily risen to throw out quislings and fifth columnists and drive back English invaders. In their minds and hearts they loathed the idea of being united with the English. They were outraged to see it happen and were fifty years in settling down to accept it. A Kirk minister who died in mid-century declared he had never preached a sermon after 1707 without lamenting or abominating the union, and neither was he untypical of his cloth nor his sermons of an abiding topic of bitter conversation among all classes. Yet why was it only the hooligans of Edinburgh and Glasgow who had risked action? Why, when the clans twice came out of the Highlands in 1715 and 1745 and registered initial successes against the troops of the hated new order, did so few other Scots join them and strike a blow to be free of it?

Part of the answer has been given in the story. They were paralysed by fear of the outcome if they began to move – perhaps a Catholic king and their Presbyterian souls in peril. If James Stuart had been willing to swear to preserve and defend the Kirk, the story might have been different. Jacobites from the Highlands and Cameronians of the south-west could have met with another than the Devil at their head, and union might have been swept into the sea until the English effected it by conquest. There were, of course, other possible kings besides James. Had Hamilton been less of a breaking reed, there might again have been another story for a while. Nor were kings entirely indispensable. The Kirk had developed its own democracy and the Scots could have tried republicanism if enough of them had had a will to it as the way out. The will was absent because the ruling classes could not risk political democracy and maintenance of the social and political hierarchy required a king at its head. The lesson of Charles I's execution had not been forgotten.

Certainly there were brakes holding back the Scots. But, if the rage and anguish at being absorbed into England had gone as deep and been as great as the Scots pretended, it is inconceivable that they would not have hit out for freedom come what might, as they had done in the past. Admittedly leaders were lacking, for the ablest men were among or with the twenty-six. And yet, if enough Scots had thought freedom worth dying for, would no Wallace or Bruce have been thrown up in the struggle? It is difficult to believe that the breed had entirely died out. As it was, only a scullion boy died, at the hand of a madman.

The brakes did not come off because the events took place in the eighteenth and not the fourteenth or the sixteenth century. The Scots lived in a small and materially untouched pocket of the new world that had been developing since the Renaissance, the discovery of routes to the east and the Americas, and the possibilities these opened up of colonisation and trade. But they were not unconscious of it, as is evidenced by the national excitement over the plunge into the Darien scheme. They were aware that they were being left behind and for the first time in their history were beginning to think that the English had something they had not and ought to have, something they could not secure by a raid across the border but only by becoming members of the new world. The full realisation of the need was confined to a few, but a dim consciousness of it was penetrating everywhere, even into the Highlands, where chiefs and their sons and nephews were not all untravelled. Scotland herself was removed from the world, but in the previous hundred years plenty of adventurous Scots had been seeing how it was developing and tasting its excitement.

The passage of time had had other effects. The lowland Scots had lost a lot of their zest for fighting in the nearly twenty years of peaceful living which had come with William and Mary after the torments endured under Charles and James and, although it had seemed to be the Englishness of these two kings that had made them bloody tyrants to the Scots, at the back of their minds they knew that the peace they were appreciating derived from the connection with England against which they were kicking. They knew too that if it were broken they would never experience the same peace again. They had to reconcile patriotism and pacifism and were encouraged towards the latter by another of the factors which cut them off somewhat from the world. In the fourteenth century, when all men were Catholics, they could leap unhesitatingly to arms as Scots. Now they had to think what would happen to their Presbyterianism if they fought. In the last hundred and fifty years Kirk and country had become almost inseparable, but if a separation could not be avoided their first loyalty must be to the Kirk. Presbyterianism had developed too an individualism of the spirit and a critical cast of mind which had freed the Scot from the unthinking claims of emotional patriotism. His own fate in the hereafter was a degree or two more important to him than his country's in this vale of sin and woe, and he had learned to ask questions before responding to his own or others' impulses. He could hate the English and join others in a jingoistic chorus of execration, but he could ask himself in the silence of the night what were the interests of his soul and of his body; and when the Kirk finally told him his soul and its own could be safe with England he was not ungrateful that his body might be safer also.

The spell which held the Scots in 1707, 1715 and 1745 lay in the depths of their national subconsciousness, where they accepted that their physical and material welfares demanded a close link with the English, that in the world of the eighteenth century it was no longer possible or sensible for the two halves of the British island to stay apart. They ranted and raved against union, but when it was offered and the twenty-six set out to push them into it, they were powerless to take any effective steps inside or outside parliament to frustrate it because they felt themselves drawn into the grip of a destiny from which they neither could nor really wanted to escape.

The English on the other hand had no mystic feelings about uniting with the Scots. In so far as most of them felt anything at all, it was a mild relief to have got rid of a shadow at their backs, if they could really be sure it would stay away. One could never trust these Scotch. A business bargain had been made – some cash, sixty seats in parliament, and a permit for Scots to get what trade they could, in exchange for allowing shackles to be put on their wrists. The universal hope was that the sixty would not make a nuisance of themselves and the rest would stay at home. The general view was that, whatever England had gained, the Scots had made her pay a high price for it, as is indicated in a broadside published in London on the date on which union took effect. It consists of four columns of satirical verse illustrated by highly elaborated sketches of types of the day – squires and ladies, politicians, clergymen, lawyers, merchants, dandies, poets, soldiers, yokels and milkmaids – all swarming round an ass on whose back some of them have climbed. It is entitled *The Ass-age, or The World in Heiroglyphick. An Amusement agreeably Resembling the Humour of the Present Time.*

> 'Poets before have brought upon the Stage
> The Leaden, Iron, and the Golden Age:
> Then why (since everything may have its day)
> May we not bring the ASS-AGE into play?
> For sure no time has ever shewn in print
> An Age with half so many Asses in't'

run the opening lines, and after describing some of the follies of the time, the broadside refers to a sly-faced man whose head and shoulders poke in from the side as he studies the scene with upraised, half-affrighted hands and a knowing grin:

> 'Sawney peeps in, in Hopes; but when he spies
> Such numbers crowding round the Ass, he cries,
> Nay, if so many English striving be
> To ride, I find there'll be no Room for me:
> But 'tis but Right we give 'em Pref'rence here;
> We made 'em buy the Union pretty dear.'

And so the English went on their way, most of them forgetting for the next hundred years – except briefly in 1715 and 1745 – that there had ever been a union or that the Scots even existed. From time to time a Scot in London made himself more than usually obnoxious and they retaliated with shouts of 'Scotch, go home!' and passed something through parliament to annoy them in the north, but by and large the two peoples lived their separate lives. England was England and grew richer and more assured, Scotland remained Scotland and poor. The United Kingdom was for parliamentary and diplomatic use only, and two-thirds of the century passed before the promised benefits of union began to be evident in the north. Trade was slow in developing and the English did nothing to help it. They did not positively hinder adventurous Scots, however, and in a decade or two some were making money in the hire of the once abused English East India Company, spreading through the colonies and adding to them as soldiers, pioneers and administrators. The cattle trade flourished. Glasgow throve on the tobacco trade. Capital became available and banks routed it to farming and manufacturing experiments. For fifty years progress was barely perceptible, but in the sixties, seventies and eighties it gained momentum. The Scots discovered to their surprise that there must have been something in union after all and gave up their national mourning. They were still no readier than the English to obey Queen Anne's injunction to show the world they had hearts disposed to become one people, but they abandoned their 'braid Scots' and began to learn to speak and write English.

The chief men who propelled the Scots into union died in their own beds. Hamilton, Belhaven and Lockhart of Carnwath had less comfortable ends.

Grateful Queen Anne made Queensberry Duke of Dover, Marquis of Beverley, Earl of Ripon, joint keeper of the Privy Seal, a Secretary of State in the United Kingdom government, and gave him a pension of £3 000 a year. He did not enjoy his reward long, but died in 1711. Seafield got a pension of £3 000 a year, was made Keeper of the Great Seal of Scotland, for which some uses were still to be found, and a United Kingdom Privy Councillor. He sat in the House of Lords as an elected Scottish peer until 1727 and died in 1730. Argyll was made Baron Chatham, Earl and later Duke of Greenwich, won fame as a soldier (which caused him to fall out with Marlborough), commanded the British forces in Spain, assisted smartly in getting George I on the throne, put down the Jacobite rebellion in 1715 and ran Scotland for the London government until he died in 1743. He was buried in Westminster Abbey and given a monument in Poets' Corner; he was no poet, but had helped to write the ending to an old song. William Carstares, who was primarily responsible for the Kirk's indispenable support of union, got a silver medal. He was only a commoner, of course. The Earl of Mar – hunchback 'Bobbing John' – got less than he felt he deserved. He had to wait until 1713 before the Tories gave him a Secretaryship of State, so as Anne's death approached he intrigued with her brother in France. When the Whigs snatched the crown for George he tried to gain his favour, was spurned and went off in 1715 to the Highlands to raise the standard for James. Balked by Argyll at Sheriffmuir, he fled to France, where he played a double game for the next ten years, hatching Jacobite plots and betraying them to the English until 1725, when he had become too disreputable to have a further part to play even in the dirty politics of his day. He died in 1732 nostalgically but happily drawing architectual plans for the improvement of the Edinburgh he could not visit. Atholl switched places with Mar. Having failed to prevent union he decided to make the most of it. In three years he won election to the House of Lords and two years later the astonished Kirk found him turning up at their General Assembly as the queen's representative. When Mar headed the Jacobites in 1715, their old leader took the field in a small way for George and captured Rob Roy MacGregor, but characteristically hedged the family bet by allowing his three sons to campaign on the other side. He gained nothing from his further efforts to keep in with the union government, but when he died in 1724 the estates were intact.

Belhaven died within a year of union of an inflamation of the brain, while out on bail from the London gaol to which he had been committed on suspicion of being involved in an abortive French invasion. In March 1708 French ships with troops and the Pretender on board suddenly appeared in the Firth of Forth and then hurried off home again to escape an English fleet. Anti-unionists including Belhaven were imprisoned and charged with inviting the French to upset the union. Belhaven was anti-union but too true a Scot to hand his country to the French. He was sent to London, where the Privy Council listened sceptically to his protests of innocence and committed him for trial. His death was ascribed to wounded patriotic pride. Lockhart of Carnwath's impudent enjoyment of being a Scots Jacobite among the English M.P.s terminated in 1715, when he was locked up to keep him out of the rebellion. Released without trial after it was over, he acted as confidential linkman between the Court of St Germains and other Jacobites until he fled to the Continent, where he was killed in a duel in 1731.

The Duke of Hamilton's end was as dramatic and mysterious as had been his behaviour at the critical moments of the union debates. The Tory ministry which brought him back into public life appointed him the queen's ambassador to restore friendly relations with Louis XIV after the Peace of Utrecht. He had become involved in a law-suit with an English peer, Lord Mohun, and on the eve of his departure for Paris in 1712 they fought a duel in Hyde Park. Hamilton killed Mohun but was wounded and then, it was alleged, received from Mohun's second, General MacCartney, another wound, from which he died. MacCartney fled but returned later to stand trial for murder and was acquitted. From which wound the Duke actually died was never established, leaving a question mark over him to the last. The belief was that the Tory inner ring were sending him to Paris to help in the coup they were planning to enable them to put James on the throne when Anne died. Whether he would have failed them as he failed the Scots is beyond knowing, and in any case the coup collapsed.

Nobody has ever learned precisely why he let the Scots down so badly. It may have been the character of the man. He was unable when the moment of action came to commit himself to the course he had recommended, was full of the sound and fury of leadership but lacked the courage to pass the point of no return. Vanity and ambition demanded he play a part which would single him out from all other men, but he could never decide on the climax of the role. Applause was to be won by being vehemently pro-Scots and anti-English, but his English estates might be at risk. It was distinctive to be Jacobite when Queensberry was pro-Hanover, but he never stepped beyond the fringes of the conspiracies and intrigues. His own pretensions to royal blood called for a degree of detachment from both houses and being known as a Jacobite required him sometimes to seem to lean to Hanover. He was probably never sincere in his opposition to union. It was a means of focussing the limelight on himself. He was no doubt as convinced as Queensberry that if the Scots were ever to have any jam on their bannocks it would have to come from England, and when he might have kept the countries apart, or at least delayed the union, he allowed the chance to pass because he could not make up his mind how much or how little or what kind of jam he wanted on his own bread.

Poor William Paterson, whose Darien scheme claims had been overlooked when the Equivalent was being distributed, and whom the Scottish parliament had recommended on its death-bed to Queen Anne, failed to get anything out of her. She did not feel personally indebted to him and his schemes had made him more enemies than friends in London. Six years of persistent urging of his case won him in 1713 a House of Commons majority for an award of £18 000, but the House of Lords threw it out. Anne had to die before he found a friend powerful enough to wear opposition down. A bill for the award was presented again in the Lords with George I's personal support and went through as one of the first grand gestures of the new reign. George was grateful for the union and Paterson was almost alone in having received no recognition of the help he had given behind the scenes in putting it through.

11 A Successful Experiment

The men who united the kingdoms and the parliaments have remained unhonoured and unsung. Only Godolphin has found any real place in history, for reasons not specially connected with that achievement. The explanation is obvious from the story here told. The circumstances of the birth of the United Kingdom were shabby. Louis XIV forced the wedding and the couple had no joy in each other or in the child. There are no heroic deeds to be commemorated, no glories are particularly connected with the event, nothing has obtained a place in the popular mind. 1603 is thought of as the date when the border vanished and the old wars ceased. 1707 stirred no emotions in the last two hundred years until some Scots of today started agitating for the bargain then made to be amended, perhaps ended.

Yet the treaty negotiators ought to have had a niche in the hall of fame while the British Empire still survived for the part they played in establishing the base from which it developed. As G. M. Trevelyan says: 'The British Empire became much greater and in every sense richer than an English Empire could ever have been with Scotland for enemy – in arms, in commerce, in colonisation, in thought, science, letters and song.' Secure from behind, the English could extend into the world as they wished. Adventurous Scots needed no longer seek service with foreign rulers. Able at last to go wherever the English went, they generously added their own brand of brain, brawn, determination and integrity to the building of empire under one crown, one flag, one parliament, one loyalty and sense of purpose. On every page in the record of the eighteenth, nineteenth and twentieth centuries, in every respect in which the British have contributed during that time for good or ill to human development, experience and knowledge, Scots names stand side by side with

English in high proportion for a country with one-tenth the population.

The Scots benefited enormously from the union. Whatever economic progress they might eventually have been able to make on their own, it would have been much less and much slower than it has been without a border. Continuing to speak and write their own vernacular, without the advantages of every kind they have enjoyed through their access to everything within England and developed by the English, they might have done as well domestically, and as members of the world community, as, say, the Danes – perhaps better in the heyday of coal and iron. They would not have enjoyed anything like the power, prestige and glory in which they have shared as co-makers of a great empire and tradition.

They had the best of both worlds. In 1707 they exchanged a kingdom and a parliament for a profitable partnership in an empire, and managed to preserve at the same time probably everything that was worth keeping of their nationhood and their soul. They have had, if they wished them, most of the advantages of being English and have remained – to the English, to themselves, and to most of the rest of the world – recognisably Scots. While very absorbable for most of the last two hundred years, they have never been absorbed by the English. They owe this in some degree to the tolerant indifference which the English have shown towards them at most times throughout the union, but primarily to the articles in the treaty which allowed them to keep their own systems of law and education and their own national church. For more than two and a half centuries they have had of necessity their own judges and lawyers, their own teachers, and their own ministers of religion, and the whole administrative apparatus and personnel required to sustain these. By means of them they have erected an invisible border which the English have not dared (or wished) to pass, and behind which generation after generation of men and women have been born and bred with a core of Scottishness that stays hard and pure wherever they wander.

The Scots should be grateful, therefore, to Queensberry, Argyll, Seafield, Stair, Mar, Marchmont, Seton of Pitmedden and the others of the twenty-six commissioners who negotiated the treaty of union with England and forced it on their own resisting nation. They should have a kind thought for Belhaven, Fletcher of Saltoun, and even Hamilton, Atholl and George Lockhart of Carnwath, without whose opposition the twenty-six might have shown less wisdom in their negotiating than they did. The English cannot be expected to honour the memory of Scots but they should not altogether forget their own commissioners, who had the sense to give the Scots terms on which they could unite, perhaps not without some loss of pride, face and voice, but without losing character and soul. The motives of the Scots commissioners and their parliamentary supporters were not patriotically pure and disinterested. Their hopes of personal or family gain undoubtedly steeled them to endure the abuse and lamentations of the nation that saw them as its ravishers. Some of them may have been susceptible to bribery. However, in so far as they were swayed by the benefits to be derived from economic union with England, they were not perverse in equating the national interest with their own. Their good proved in course of time to have been the national good on both sides of the border.

In recent years Scottish nationalists have agitated for the United Kingdom to be broken up, for Scotland to separate again from England and be given back her parliament and in- dependence. Other Scots have expressed a desire to see a parlia- ment in Edinburgh again, but dealing only with domestic affairs and leaving foreign affairs and defence to a federal parliament at Westminster. This is no place to enter into a discussion of these proposals. It may be that the union could now be given a federal form which was impossible in 1707. It would be a sad thing if two peoples, whom God, geography and two and a half centuries of a great history have joined together, were to separate and the United Kingdom were to be no more. The last words of this story should be those of G. S. Pryde, a shrewd Scots historian, as he summed it up in 1950. 'The entire record of human affairs,' he declared, 'shows nothing really comparable to the agreement, made without conquest and observed for over two hundred and forty years, of two very unequal peoples to form one state but to remain two nations. ... The practical question of its full relevance to mid-twentieth century conditions need not be confused with the historical assessment of its past contribution to the welfare of Britain. No change made hereafter should be the occasion for reviling those who in 1706–7 did what seemed to them to be best for the two countries, or for regretting what has been a noble, unique, and on the whole remarkably successful experiment.'

BOOKS WHICH MAY BE CONSULTED

Contemporary Records

History of the Union of Great Britain. By Daniel Defoe. (Edinburgh, 1709.) Another edition, with other papers on the subject by Defoe, was published in London in 1786 under the title *History of the Union between England and Scotland.*

After the signing of the Treaty of Union in 1706 Defoe was sent to Edinburgh by Robert Harley, one of Godolphin's Secretaries of State, to report to him on the progress of the treaty through the Scottish parliament and other relevant happenings. An enthusiast for union, Defoe assisted the Queensberry administration in every way open to him. He provides an admirably detailed account of proceedings inside and outside parliament and is specifically informative on the economic and commercial aspects of the treaty.

The Lockhart Papers: containing memoirs and commentaries upon the affairs of Scotland from 1702 to 1715 by George Lockhart of Carnwath. From original manuscripts in the possession of A. Aufrere. (London, 1817.)

George Lockhart writes as a Jacobite opponent of union about the personalities and the intrigues. He had a rare gift for the observation of character and faithfully records the merits of his enemies and the faults of his friends.

Memoirs of the Secret Services of J. Macky, Esq. during the Reigns of King William, Queen Anne, and King George I, including also the True Secret History of the Rise, Promotions, Etc. of the English and Scots Nobility, Officers Civil, Military, and Naval, and Other Persons of Distinction from the Revolution. Edited by A. R. (London, 1733.)

John Macky was a Scot employed by London govern-

191

ments to watch the moves and movements of Jacobites in France and England. He assiduously assembled dossiers of information about all persons of distinction. He was as strong for union as Lockhart was against it. As he had also a detective's matter-of-fact eye for character and appearance, while Lockhart was more of a romantic and psychologist, their observations on personalities are usefully complementary.

Statutory Instruments

The texts of the following acts of the two parliaments are to be found in *English Historical Documents,* Vol. VIII, 1660–1714. (Eyre and Spottiswoode, London, 1953.)

Act anent Peace and War (Scottish parliament, 1703);

Act for the Security of the Kingdom (Scottish parliament, 1704);

Act for an Union of the Two Kingdoms (English parliament, 1707), incorporating :

> The Articles of the Treaty of Union as passed by the Scottish Parliament, 1707;

> Act for Securing the Protestant Religion and Presbyterian Church Government within the Kingdom of Scotland (Scottish parliament, 1706);

> Act for Securing the Church of England as by Law Established (English parliament, 1707);

> Act for Settling the Manner of Electing the Sixteen Peers and Forty-five Members to Represent Scotland in the Parliament of Great Britain (Scottish parliament, 1707).

Twentieth-century Histories

Scotland and the Union : *a history of Scotland from 1695 to 1747.* By William Law Mathieson. (James Maclehose and Sons, Glasgow, 1905.)

England under Queen Anne. Vol. II *Ramillies and the Union of Scotland.* By G. M. Trevelyan, O.M. (Longmans, London, 1930–34.)

Commentaries

Thoughts on the Union between England and Scotland. By A. V. Dicey and R. S. Rait. (Macmillan and Co., London, 1920.)

The Treaty of Union of Scotland and England, 1707. Edited, with an introduction, by George S. Pryde. (Nelson, London, 1950.)

Social Background

A History of the Scottish People, 1560–1830. By T. C. Smout. (Collins, London, 1969.)

INDEX